D0368700

ALL THINGS

AND

STUFF

To Mrs. Trainer

May these pages be a blessing -

Ruth Y. Hackman

ALL THINGS

AND

STUFF

Ruth Y. Hackman

FLEMING H. REVELL COMPANY
WESTWOOD, NEW JERSEY

Verses from the publications *Living Letters, Living Prophecies,* and *Living Gospels* appear by permission of Tyndale House Publishers, Wheaton, Illinois.

Scripture quotations identified by KJV are from the *King James Version of the Bible.*

TO MY HUSBAND WALTER
AND OUR FIVE CHILDREN
Rosie
  Becky
    Jenny
     Joe
       Libby

PREFACE

This book was conceived in reality and born in reality.

I wrote these pages to the rhythm of my washer and dryer, with a backdrop of drying sheets. In full view of my writing table were two baskets with ironing, rising in height as the manuscript grew.

Many of the quotes from my children were written in two note books which I called my "gem books," and were collected over a period of years. My only regret is that I did not start my "gem books" sooner. I do not have many available quotes from my three oldest daughters: Rosie, Becky and Jenny; not because they didn't talk, but the things children say are soon forgotten unless they are recorded.

It is my firm belief that children say what we feel, only in more understandable and honest language.

It was my husband who insisted that I accept the challenge of writing this book, and kept encouraging me when I wasn't sure I would make it.

My son, Joe, was my most valuable critic. I depended on his judgment for every page. If he said, "I don't get it," I knew the procedure I must follow. Rewrite!

It was kind of Kenneth Taylor to grant me permission to quote from *Living Letters, Living Gospels,* and *Living Prophecies.*

I owe many thanks to Mrs. Thelma Thomas, who so ably typed the manuscript, and also to friends who gave me their stories to share in the book.

As I wrote *All Things and Stuff,* I prayed many times that I would write the words that your heart would need.

Allentown, Pennsylvania   RUTH Y. HACKMAN

CONTENTS

VIEWPOINT

. . . we will keep me!

"All Things and Stuff"

One night Joey was praying, and to cover a lot of territory quickly, he prayed for "all things and stuff." It isn't very flattering when a child can reflect one's prayers in a few words. Had I given the impression that prayer takes too much time to be specific?

I have prayed for the missionaries around the world. I wouldn't want to miss anyone. I have prayed for the hungry and needy, only to wake up the next day stuffing myself with many more calories than the daily requirement. I have thanked the Lord for food, shelter, and clothing, merely using a trite phrase to fill up the time. I have called, "Come on, let's hurry and have family worship," as though it were something to be endured.

I ask God for this and that: "Be with me tomorrow. . . . Give me a good night's sleep. . . . Lead, guide, and direct us. . . . Help me to overcome temptation. . . . Help me to be a witness. . . . I pray that we might all (our family) remain true and faithful to Thee till Thou dost come. . . . Lord use us to Thy name's honor and glory."

I have used these phrases so many times, over and over, again and again. I could say them without thinking.

I remember when I prayed, "Now I lay me . . . and God bless Mommie and Daddy, sister, Grandma and Grandpa, Uncle . . . ." I prayed this prayer with such rigidness and regularity that it was like an obsession. If I made a mistake in any way, I would start at the beginning. I repeated this procedure many times. According to the psychologist of today, I must have been a disturbed child. Fortunately for me, my parents didn't understand psychology.

Hanging my prayers on the line to air, I have come to the

conclusion that I have not put away childish things. Many of my prayers could easily be summed up as "all things and stuff."

"Green's My Friend"

Joe liked anything green. My green dress was his favorite. His bedspread was green, and his fuzzy blanket was green.

He described it so clearly, one day, when he said, "Green's my friend."

You can't improve on the words children use to express themselves. When you say, "I like green," or "I love green," it doesn't create nearly the warmth, as when you say, "Green's my friend."

It is regrettable that we so often insist on our children talking like adults. They can create pictures with a few words, that we cannot produce in a paragraph.

I didn't remember the incident, but Joe was trying to refresh my memory by saying, "That time I was crying and the man was trying to tame me." The word *tame* brings that whole sentence to life. I can see a screaming, kicking boy, with a man trying to subdue him bodily. Joey chose that word spontaneously, without a thesaurus or a dictionary.

Thomas à Kempis said: "God walketh with the simple, revealeth himself to the humble, giveth understanding to the little ones."

It is a pity that children cannot write books, for we adults cannot match their originality. I wish I had created "Green's my friend."

If you keep your ear tuned to the conversation of children, you will know why Jesus enjoyed their company, and why he said, ". . . for of such is the kingdom of heaven" (MATTHEW 19:14, KJV).

The Whale's Side of the Story

One day, Joe was telling the story of Jonah and the whale, with paper bag puppets. I was surprised to hear him tell it from the whale's point of view. "What an experience for me," he said, "to swallow a man whole! I usually chop them up."

It helps to change your vantage point. Looking at things from a different angle will give you an entirely new dimension. There was always the whale's side of the story. I had never thought about it.

How could I have been so narrow in my thinking all these years, and thought only of poor Jonah? That must have been a dreadful three days for that whale, as he bounced up and down on those giant white caps. In fact, he finally got so seasick, he regurgitated Jonah on dry land.

Joe's puppet show has set me thinking. We need some of this logic. That character you met at the laundromat, who snapped at you when you asked her for change, in her unkind answer was really trying to tell you, "I'm tired . . . had a terrible night . . . no sleep . . . three children not waiting their turn to vomit. The linen closet is empty . . . feel half sick myself."

If only we could know the reason for actions and reactions. We were camping at our church camp, gawking at a family near us. The woman carried the children and seemed to take the lead in everything. I began judging the man as being a lazy, shiftless, good-for-nothing husband.

We went on a hike later and that poor woman was again plaguing herself with those children. I hope she didn't hear me remarking about it! She turned and said so sweetly, "You know my husband feels so self-conscious that he can't help with the children, but he has been very ill. These children are my nieces and nephews. We enjoy taking them with us." For that minute, I wished I could have been a prairie dog and crawled in a hole.

I should have known there was the whale's side of the story.

"My Daddy . . . Hunts Mice!"

The story of Jim Elliott (one of five missionaries martyred in Ecuador) is a fascinating one. After reading the book about him, we were discussing the way Jim disciplined himself, even in high-school and college days. He would run around the track for exercise, and choose his foods carefully to build up a rugged body for missionary work in the future.

Our five-year-old son was listening, and not willing to have his daddy outdone by anyone he announced, "My daddy is a hunter!" Since his daddy didn't so much as own a gun, we listened, and Joe continued seriously, "He hunts mice!"

Poor Daddy! What a let down!

We all laughed, but Joe must have been puzzled. Wasn't David Livingston a missionary hunter? What's so funny about hunting mice? Doesn't Mother scream, holler, and shake, when she sees one of those horrible creatures? She slams the door and screams even if it's a dead mouse in the trap. There couldn't be much more commotion around the house if a Bengal tiger had suddenly made his appearance on the scene. Of course, Daddy's the hero.

Only an adoring little son would label a man a hunter, when the small game he hunts are mice.

"... So Many Ketchups"

Life gets more complicated every day. Even our first-grader knows what it's all about. One day, after watching television, she declared, "There are so many ketchups on TV, I don't know which one is the good one."

If it were only ketchups! But how do I know I'm using the best laundry soap? That name-brand piano I looked at the other night—would I be paying for the name, do you think? If I should decide on the better trademark, I have the choice between the baby grand or the console type, or the thirty-six inch sounding board spinet against the forty-five inch sounding board studio model. When it is not pianos, it is the more important decisions, where you don't have as much choice.

Would it be right for me to sell something I don't approve of, using the argument, "I don't want to be another person's conscience?" Should I report a teacher who uses suggestive language in his classroom, even at the expense of involving my child, who is in this teacher's class? Is it merely a true or false question, as to whether my radio commercials must be completely honest?

I don't know my intelligence quotient, but many times it takes more knowledge than I have to decide, "Which one is the good one?"

Line by Line

Yesterday, Libby came home with *very good* stamped on her "First Grade News" sheet. The paper was unusually well done. Copying the newspaper had become quite a chore for her, until yesterday, when the teacher used a new method.

"She wrote a line, and we wrote a line," Libby commented. "Do you like that better?" I asked. "Yeah, you get it over with then." Libby is learning more than just writing. She is learning a basic essential to a happy life.

When I begin the day and view all the work that must be done as one big confusing *page*, I lose heart. I retain my sanity only when I resign myself to tackling it job by job. We lose precious time when we agonize over the immensity of our tasks.

I remind myself, while writing this book, that I cannot keep counting the pages I have yet to do. I must write it line by line, and be thankful for every page that is done.

Life is like a difficult puzzle. The whole jumbled mass of intricate pieces can baffle us, until we condition our minds that the only possible way to assemble it is piece by piece. As Charlie Brown says, "Happiness is finding the piece with the pink edge and part of the sky and the top of a sailboat." We don't learn this fact in one easy lesson. It is difficult to accept, since we are so eager to get things done with speed.

But there is a real feeling of accomplishment when we face our difficult situations, job by job, piece by piece, line by line.

"A Christian-Mennonite Crack-Up"

One day, Joe reported to me that there had been "a Christian-Mennonite crack-up"—an accident in which some Mennonite folks were involved. Because we were both Christians and Mennonites, Joe probably thought we might be interested, and we were. If Joe continues his news reporting, however, he will need to learn a few things. The implications of a report like this are endless.

As the reporter, he could be charged with discrimination: the future business dealings of the victim might be affected and his freedom hampered. The exposure of religious affiliation might influence a jury. I'm glad Joe didn't reveal whether a male or female had been driving the vehicle; such information could bring charges of defamation of character! Good reporting should give no indication of a person's sex, color, nationality, or religion. In many instances, not even the name should be mentioned; there might be unfavorable reflection on the family and loss of prestige! Serious consideration should be given to disclosure of the name of a car involved. Reflection on any particular model could draw strong protest from the manufacturer!

After I get it through Joe's head that he must be more careful in what he reports, he will probably fume: "OK, Mom, OK. Forget that there ever was an accident!"

As Charlie Brown says, "Good grief!"

"... Halloween, Thanksgiving, Christmas, and Easter"

Today, the school children celebrated Halloween. A little bunny and a masked baseball player got on the bus together. The suspense and excitement was enhanced by the heavy frost that was surely on the pumpkin.

Several weeks ago, Libby remarked, "I can hardly wait for Halloween, Thanksgiving, Christmas, and Easter." In other words, the whole year looked exciting to her. We covet the enthusiasm of children—their eagerness and indefatigability—but children too can lose their fervor.

One Valentine's Day, Becky came home from school with an armload of valentines. She didn't seem to care about them;

some were not even opened. That evening she became very ill. As I sat and watched her through the night, I knew the reason for her apathy toward her valentines. Feeling well has so much to do with how we react to almost everything.

There are days when my house seems just right. I am happy and contented. If I have a day with a headache, however, my kitchen is too small and the hardwood floors would look much better with wall to wall carpet. My poor husband and children also become prey to my critique.

If our headaches or backaches come from sources that we cannot control, I believe God understands our discontentment. "For he knoweth our frame; he remembereth that we are dust" (PSALMS 103:14, KJV).

Unless you are a hypochondriac, you will want to thank God for every day that you can say, "I can hardly wait for Halloween, Thanksgiving, Christmas, and Easter."

"... Save It for My Marriage"

One morning before leaving for school, Libby asked, "Do I have to make my bed today?" "Are you getting tired of it?" I questioned. "I want to save it for my marriage," she reasoned. Where does a six-year-old get the idea that making beds after you're married is more desirable?

Marriage is not a power that will turn a girl into a housewife by a wave from a magic wand, nor will it turn a boy into the breadwinner over night. The big difference they expected to feel as they walked from the altar, does not exist; even pinching yourself doesn't help. Just saying *I do* will not kindle the desire to make beds.

The majority of our children will become husbands and wives, mothers and fathers. We encourage them through sixteen or twenty years of school to become teachers or engineers, yet we leave them to enter marriage with so little knowledge and know-how.

He may have a master's degree, but does he know how to compliment a wife for a good dinner? Has she ever done any family shopping? If not, a supermarket with all its cans and packages of various sizes and labels, can mean a frustrated wife. To choose between fresh or frozen, canned or dried, price or quality, can cause a novice to lose her equilibrium.

Saving too much to learn until after marriage will mean cramming. Under this tension, it's no wonder many flunk the test.

"We Will Keep Me!"

Our family was talking about having another baby, when our youngest declared, "If we get another baby, we will keep me!" It wasn't a question but a statement.

Me is always important. A child clutches a toy and says, "Mine." It may not be a complete sentence as far as sentence structure is concerned, but it's a complete sentence in the area of communication.

It's hard for us to get out of the spotlight. We've had a good time there. Admirers have fallen at our feet. We speak, others obey. We get special benefits because of our position. The threat of losing status causes us to exert *me* all over the place.

There are some of us who use soft sell in trying to attract attention, and others use hard sell. One way is scarcely more virtuous than the other. Soft sell might be more tactful.

I cook, bake, and sew hoping someone will ask, "Did you bake this?" or "Did you make that?" Their "oh's" and "ah's" are just what *me* needs.

We may appear very generous, giving out this, handing away that. We know in our hearts if our motives are right. The extreme love of self can actually become a god to us, dominating our whole lives.

It's frightening to think that *me* would try to compete with God.

"*Tell Me When You're Sleeping*"

The doors were checked, the prayers were said, the kisses were given, and I was just getting settled for the night. I was hoping the rest were too, when Libby Lou called, "Tell me when you're sleeping."

Bedtime and sleep are experiences most children think they could do without. I suppose Libby thought if she had to go through with it, knowing she had company would help. She was not aware of the fact that I couldn't tell her when I was sleeping. Sleep is an individual matter, and we go through it alone.

I was scheduled for an operation on my nose. Any operation where there is the possibility of cancer, even skin cancer, is not the type of thing we enjoy.

Friends said: "Don't worry. . . . You'll be all right. . . . I have a friend who had the same thing. . . . I have a small spot on my nose too."

There was one person, I felt, who understood. His family visited with our family all through our childhood years; now he came to me as a pastor. He had just gone through a stay in the hospital himself, and it was still vivid in his mind.

In essence, this is what he said, "No other person can go through this for you. When the time comes, you will face the operation alone. It will be your very own experience."

That was what I needed. Now it seemed more like a venture than a duplication of what happens to everyone else.

The incoherent speech of someone talking in his sleep only makes us realize how alone we really are. We can only talk about the benefits of sleep when we wake up and stretch. It is only then we can realize the blessings the Lord had in mind.

"You'll Have To Hunt Your Nuts"

Jenny was so eager to forget about her studies, during a few weeks of vacation, that she said, "I'm going to hibernate." Libby was listening and scoffed, "Well, then you'll have to hunt your nuts." She was probably thinking about the little chipmunks she fed popcorn to on our camping trips last summer.

I feel sorry for the healthy, capable folks who think only of the day they can retire. They scarcely enjoy the present, dreaming about their retirement years. In this period of life known as retirement, a sense of worth must be maintained. A complete departure from the former life can be disastrous. To suddenly realize that your former job is being carried on and you are not being missed, is quite a blow to your ego.

Sleeping as long as you want to, is not nearly as exciting as you thought it would be. After a few weeks of this kind of snoozing, you long for a reason to get up. You still need activity, you still need people. To feel valuable, you must do something valuable. Hobbies alone do not satisfy this craving.

You understand of course, that I am not talking from experience, just from observation, so you are not obliged to take my advice. I think, however, to look forward to a selfish retirement, and plan only for what you yourself will enjoy, can bring only frustration.

A far better attitude would be that of a friend of mine who said, "I hope I can be like a violin string that plays until it snaps."

We do not have the physical capacities and instincts for hibernation. It is alien to us. That's why Libby admonished, "Well, then you'll have to hunt your nuts."

"... *Save It for Lincoln's Birthday*"

Jenny is very fussy about what she wears for certain occasions. What she wears must complement the occasion. She must *feel* what she wears. Even when a small child, she manifested this characteristic.

It was the week of February the twelfth. I told Jenny to put on a clean nightie before she went to bed. Jenny replied, "Oh, Mother, I thought I wanted to save it for Lincoln's Birthday." Sentimental Jenny, as I sometimes call her. Jenny hates to give up clothes. Her clothes seem to be part of her. Maybe it's because she was a slow-growing child and wore the same ones for so many seasons. Her lavender baptism dress with her lavender Testament to match are fondly packed away with her memoirs.

Men are sentimental about clothes too, even though they would never admit it. Why do men react so violently when that "perfectly good hat" is thrown away. It's not because they can't afford a new one; they probably have one already, but there is emotion and feeling bound up in that deformed piece of felt. It has brought confidence and warmth. The hat has been worn for courting and fishing. It has been protection from the beating sun and the driving rain. To a man, it represents endurance and stability. Without this hat, he loses his sense of security.

Only the folks with well-seasoned clothes know what I'm talking about. If you have a wardrobe with a personality, you don't need more than a clean pair of pajamas to celebrate Lincoln's Birthday.

HONESTY

I don't too!

Self-Portrait

Joey, Libby, and I were waiting for broadcast time in a local radio station. To pass the time constructively, Libby was drawing a picture of the studio room we were in. She had the swinging mike, the telephone, and the acoustic tile on the ceiling. On one chair she had me standing, because she doesn't know how to draw a person sitting. On the other chair, where she should have drawn herself, she informed me it was Joe. "Oh," I said, "I thought that was you." "I can't be seeing the picture when I'm drawing it," she responded.

Of course! If she were part of the scene, it would be difficult to draw herself. I should have known. I suppose a person could draw a picture of himself with a mirror, but what I see in the mirror, I don't always like. I would probably be tempted to narrow the double chin, and paint out a few wrinkles in my brow or maybe the scar at my right eye. I would make myself something that I am not.

There are some folks, like the artist I knew who painted a self-portrait . . . every wrinkle, and more, were painted into that face. He underestimated his appearance.

The apostle Paul says: "As God's messenger I give each of you God's warning: be honest in your estimate of yourselves, measuring your value by how much faith God has given you" (ROMANS 12:3 LIVING LETTERS).

"I Don't Too!"

The well worn argument, of whether to say ēither or eīther, does not bother a child. Instead of saying, "I don't either," Joey declared simply, "I don't too!"

The way you prefer to say ēither or eīther, nēither or neīther is not important. The dictionary accepts both, but choose one or the other and use it consistently. It's the people who use ēither with me, and eīther with someone else who annoy me.

In this same category, I place the person with an unreal telephone voice. Her wispy "Hull—ooo" pulsates through that phone until she knows who you are, and then she changes gears.

The one characteristic I covet of my Dad, is the ability to be the same with all people. He did not feel too small to speak to important people nor too big to chat with the less fortunate. Their social standing made no difference in his ēithers or eīthers or the tone of his voice.

I was attending the annual open house at our local high school. The biology teacher, with a doctor's degree, was an interesting and capable person. As I was leaving the room, I heard her exclaim to another group of parents, "Ain't nature wonderful!" I have a feeling she would have said *ain't* to a roomful of Ph.D.'s, too.

Even though it is not good English, I'll choose the person any day who says, "I don't too," rather than the one who uses both ēither and eīther.

"Two, Big, High"

"How much do you love me?" I asked our two-year-old Libby. With her own limited vocabulary at her command, she said, "Two, big, high." I was deeply touched, because I knew those three words were the most expressive words she knew to describe her feelings. It was so real, so honest.

Like children, we should be completely honest with God. There is no advantage in being egotistical with Him. I can be conceited around strangers, but my close relatives and friends know me too well.

Many of my prayers sound like I'm praying to a stranger, to someone I am still trying to impress. If I pray publicly, I try to move the crowd, too, with my free flow of words, the uniqueness of my phrases, or my knowledge of adjectives. When I pray in private, I try to sway God with the length of my prayers, or my physical posture.

God is well acquainted with us. All he wants is our sincere and honest response. If "two, big, high" is the extent of your vocabulary, say it sincerely. God would rather hear that than any other prayer in the world.

"Same as Jane"

I picked up Libby after school and then we went for Jenny at high school. I hadn't noticed, but Jenny thought Libby seemed exceptionally quiet.

When we pulled in the lane, before we went into the house, I checked Libby's school papers. On her Modern Math paper the teacher had written these words, "Same as Jane." "Same as Jane? Libby did you copy from Jane?" I asked. With this Libby burst into tears and shook with sobs.

This was not the first time I had encountered this problem in child rearing, but that didn't make it any easier as I watched Libby sit there and cry. I tried to explain to her that I would rather she have "X's" than copy from someone else. After talking to her for a while, I told her she should ask Jesus to forgive her. Between sobs, she prayed for forgiveness, and then I prayed.

As we got out of the car I saw tears rolling down Jenny's cheeks too. Jenny was probably thinking of the time she had to go to her teachers and make similar confessions. If children only knew our feelings at a time like this! Jenny is beginning to understand I think.

I'm so grateful to Libby's teacher, because I know she cares about Libby. That "Same as Jane" paper will be saved and someday Libby will look at it—gratefully.

Don't Be an Authority

It was hunting season. Two beautiful buck deer were hanging outside the local tavern, in full view of all who passed by.

Becky was explaining to her brother, Joey, how to shoot a deer. Dramatically she stated, "They just say, 'Stick 'em up,' and then shoot!" Can you hunters picture that: giving a deer time to "stick 'em up"? Joe didn't know any better, so she was safe.

The truth was Becky had never seen a deer shot. Her daddy didn't own a gun, so hunting was hardly discussed at our house. No one is an authority because he sounds like one. It is usually the person with the least experience who has the most answers.

Unless you are sure of your audience, bluffing is a dangerous practice. It is imperative that your attender be less intelligent than you. He must not have a knowledge of your subject— he might ask embarrassing questions. You can't afford to give a spiel on how smart you are about the law, and then discover that your listener is a lawyer.

Suppose I should meet an author and not know it. I might try to display my knowledge on writing a book, only to find out I was talking to Dr. Tournier. After being deflated, one learns that the shriveled feeling is horrible. It's not worth the risk.

"For everyone who tries to honor himself shall be humbled;

and he who humbles himself shall be honored" (LUKE 14:11
LIVING GOSPELS).

Childish Honesty

Tape recorders and commercials are part of Libby's life. She said her first words on a radio spot before her second birthday. While enjoying a day off from school, Libby was pretending she was giving a commercial. She ended the spot with the closing phrase, "I like Mommie." Impulsively I gave her a hug and kiss, after which she admitted, "That was not for real, but I like you anyway."

If only adults would maintain some of this childish honesty. People today seem to have no qualms about deceiving even their close friends. What has happened to our consciences? Or is this the reason for our thriving psychiatric clinics?

A man came to our door telling me he wanted to give a first aid demonstration. I made an appointment with him for a time when my husband would be home. I should have known it was a gimmick. He was selling an expensive fire alarm system. He came into our home under false pretense.

I see the same tactics being used in churches and Christian organizations. The main feature of a program is used as a decoy, after which they "lower the boom." If we want to see how flowers are arranged, then let's have a night for flower arrangements, but let's not sneak in the evangelistic appeal at the close of the service. I don't blame folks for thinking they have been trapped. Isn't this misrepresentation?

There are too few of us who embrace our childish honesty.

We Cannot Polish the Manger

Joe and Libby were listening to a recording of the Christmas story and how the manger held the Baby Jesus. "Wouldn't you have liked to hold Baby Jesus," Joe asked. "If He would be in a house," Libby replied.

The stable scene was stark realism to Libby. She must have visualized cows and donkeys walking around, accompanied by sheep from the shepherd's flocks—surely not desirable surroundings to rock a baby.

We tend to glamorize the stable. We portray the donkey and the ox as gently accepting the new addition; the dove on the rafters as cooing the Christ Child to sleep; the clean soft hay as an ideal pillow for his head.

But Mary and Joseph found that barn real, too. The body heat of the animals and the warmed breath steaming from their nostrils created quite a humid atmosphere. The smell in the stable, mixed with the uncomfortable beads of perspiration from childbirth, is not exactly what a new mother anticipates. Even the swaddling clothes could not absorb the clean, fresh smell of a baby, because of competition.

In Libby's mind, the Christmas stable was still a stable. The donkeys kicked and the oxen had horns.

If we will understand the great sacrifice of Christ's birth and of His death, we cannot polish the manger, nor smoothly sand His cross.

Transparent Mirror Glass

Rosie and Becky were trying to explain to their grandmother about the new type of glass that was going to be installed in their Sunday-school classroom doors, "The kind where the pupils cannot see out, but others can look in." Little Jenny was listening and piped up, "I hope they get it inside out."

It does make a person uneasy to know one is exposed to the eyes of the world, anytime. People are looking in on us everyday through transparent mirror glass, and we are not conscious of it.

One's true self shows up when we think no one is looking or that no one knows us. I would be careful of shaking my fist at a driver wearing sunglasses. It might be my pastor in a new car. Early morning family feuds had better be postponed until one is sure the milkman has gone. If you must bicker with the policeman, make sure the bicycle that just passed was not ridden by your son.

We have found out in camping across the country that there are very few places we can go without finding someone we know, or who knows our boss or our next door neighbor. There are times we, too, wish the transparent mirror glass were inside out.

Though it might be possible to be out of the sight of people, there is still God, looking in.

VALUES

Naughty smart or good smart?

A Balloon for an Anchor

One day, Libby was sitting in a large zipper bag, where I store our camping blankets. She was making believe it was a boat, and, holding a balloon on a string, she explained, "This is my anchor."

In my wildest imagination, I cannot picture a balloon being used for an anchor. Right now, I cannot think of any two things being more opposite. Can you picture someone trying to anchor a boat with a balloon? One cannot get a boat anchored, if the anchor rides the waves. The anchor must go down deep, and fasten securely.

Libby is not the only one who lives in a world of fantasy, and pretends balloons are anchors. We try to find security by being successful in business, or in a profession. "Our anchorage will surely be in view," we contend, "when we move into our tri-level house in a bi-level neighborhood. Come what may, our policies, our bank accounts, and our real estate will take care of us!"

Have you, or has someone in your family, ever been deathly sick? Did you read your bank deposit book for comfort? Did you care about Wall Street and the click of ticker tape? Was the huge fire place and the wall to wall carpet any consolation as you lay in your oxygen tent? These tangible things which you considered concrete, suddenly became weightless and meaningless—even repulsive.

A sense of defeat and hopelessness sweeps over you, as you realize that with these "crazy balloons," you will never cast anchor.

"... A Personality Complex"

Near my parental home is a house that is literally by the side of the road. Being within a few feet of the road, it is in an undesirable location. In recent years, this house has been painted and redecorated many times.

We were discussing this fact on the way home from Grandmother's. With typical present day logic, Jenny analyzed, "It must have a personality complex."

It is a sad state of affairs, according to the intelligentsia, when a person is not happy with himself. The personality-complexed people spend their lives looking for ways to improve themselves. They refuse to be content with the status quo.

In sharp contrast are the mentally healthy folks, who accept themselves as they are.

I am overweight! Should I accept myself as I am, thereby revealing that I have good mental health?

A dear friend of ours finally learned to accept himself with the help of tranquilizers. Before he left for the golf course, he took a tranquilizer so he could keep calm. As he told us later, "I played lousy golf, and didn't care."

Dear Lord, deliver me from people or pills that will make me feel happy with the way I am.

Green Water, or White

On his second trip to the ocean, Joe was enjoying the waves. He soon realized that if they broke before they reached him, it meant trouble. "Daddy," he said, "I like the green water, not the white."

When I look out over the ocean, and feel the spray that is left behind, I like the white caps best.

We were camping in the Black Woods of Acadia National Park. The huge waves dashed against the rugged Maine coast making quite a spectacle. At the thunder hole, the waves actually produced a sound like the clap of thunder. However, if I had been suddenly swept into the thunder hole, I would probably say, too, "I like 'the green water, not the white.' "

I love snow. Still a child at heart, I hate to see it stop snowing. Snow transforms even the unlovely spots into fairyland. But I have never been marooned in a blizzard. Thanks to my husband and children, and now a snow blower, I have never shoveled much snow. I can sit on the warm side of the window and watch the beauty of the falling snow.

To have definite opinions, without an actual encounter with snow or waves, sickness or death, or any phase of life, is absurd.

"I like the green water, not the white," was an opinion formed in the ocean, not sitting on the bank.

The Cat in the Pail

I remember my father relating an incident that happened when I was a child.

We lived on a farm where there was a lot of activity for a small girl. One day, while going from the house to the barn (or the barn to the house), I was horrified to see a cat drinking from a pail of milk that had been left in the driveway. I went quickly, to find my father. After excitedly telling him how the cat was lapping from the pail and ruining the milk, I received an indifferent "Ah, I guess not." Frustrated, I persisted, "Well then taste it!" Contamination is not that easy to detect. My mother died at the age of twenty-four of typhoid, contracted by drinking impure water. Poison gas, that can kill you, may be odorless. Radioactivity in the air, than can cripple or maim even the unborn, is not felt or tasted.

Today we Christians see the "cat in the pail" in the religious world. Do we respond apathetically, "Ah, I guess not"? Does it bother you that religious services are conducted by men who don't believe in the existence of God?

We were baffled in our bookstore, one day, when a customer asked us for, ". . . a prayer book that's not too religious."

Do we care enough that in our colleges (including so-called Christian colleges) are some professors who undermine the basic principles of our faith that we have taught our children? We stand by, aghast, but try hard not to give the appearance of being fanatics.

"Then too," we defend, "doesn't kitty have a right to her supper?"

Writing to Myself

Our house was a sight! We were painting, papering, and sanding floors. We had all the furniture removed from the living room and dining room. The clumsy upright piano was in the kitchen, and for several days we couldn't sit down to eat.

It was really rough for our small son. I kept shouting, "Don't touch this," and "Don't touch that"; "Stay off of this," and "Watch out for that." I soon realized Joey wasn't around. I called him, expecting that he was into trouble again. He answered from upstairs, "I in bed."

A child who goes to bed of his own free will, and is not thrown into it bodily, is usually sick, wounded in spirit, or afraid to tell you something he has done.

The Bible says: "Children, obey your parents . . ." (EPHE-SIANS 6:1, LIVING LETTERS). We parents should read a few verses further where it says, "And now a word to you parents. Don't keep on scolding and nagging your children, making them angry and resentful. But bring them up with the loving discipline the Lord Himself approves, with suggestions and godly advice" (v. 4).

When I see the potential that hangs around the street corners these days, I wonder; isn't there work for these loafers to do at home? Maybe lawns to mow, dishes to wash, drawers to clean—something? Or did someone request "Will you get out of the house and let me do it," or "Scram, I don't have time to show you now"? When they return home, these victims will hear, "You've been loafing around all day again. When I was your age I did. . . ."

Joe is thirteen now and doesn't answer, "I in bed," anymore, but he read this chapter and he said, "Mother, you are writing this to yourself."

Spoiling Our Fun

Joe got a bag of rubber Indians and cannibals as a gift from his sister, Becky, so I suggested that he could be a missionary to them instead of playing war. I soon heard the bang, bang, bang, of a full scale war. I went to the doorway to check on the bombardment. He looked at me seriously and explained, "A missionary did come to them, but they didn't listen."

He had a very good argument; this would have been quite feasible. However, I know Joe very well, and I have a feeling the missionary did not want too many conversions because that would spoil the fun. If we really mean business in our Christian life it will spoil our fun.

Jesus, in the Sermon on the Mount, said, "Don't do your deeds publicly. . . . But when you do a kindness to someone, do it secretly . . ." (MATTHEW 6:1, 3, LIVING GOSPELS). That would spoil our fun! Does Christ mean that when I give a big check to the church, no one should know about it? Does He mean that when I visit the sick, I should do it inconspicuously? I certainly don't feel like knocking myself out in church work, if no one is going to hear about it.

Christ also says, "Don't store up your profits here on earth. . . . But store them in heaven . . ." (MATTHEW 6:19, 20, LIVING GOSPELS). Does He mean we should not have bank accounts? A Christian should be a good business man! If the stock market offers a wise investment, doesn't He want us to play the game?

We believe in conversion. We believe the Sermon on the Mount should be taken literally, but when it spoils our fun, we make exceptions.

"I Feel So Fresh"

Autumn: the time of the year when summer clothes feel too cool in the morning and winter clothes are too hot when school is out in the afternoon.

One day Joe came home from school and took off his long-sleeved shirt and corduroys to put on dungarees and a polo shirt. The relief was quite obvious when he remarked, "I feel so fresh."

There are some who will wear their winter togs, regardless. They insist, "It's almost Halloween and time for wools and plaids!" So rather than be comfortable, they go right on perspiring through Indian Summer.

We are so bound by routine! Just because we always did it, is not enough reason to keep doing it.

In our homes, some poor women are slaves to the traditional pattern of housework. "Going 'round the mulberry bush" has become an obsession.

This is the way we wash our clothes, so early Monday morning.

This is the way we iron our clothes, so early Tuesday morning.

This is the way we mend our clothes. . . .

I would miss many invigorating experiences if I were to follow that routine.

"This is the way we go to church," includes most of us. Traditions in the church are hard to change, too.

One group disagrees concerning whether it is preferable to kneel upright or not.

Another fellowship argues, "We always said *debts* instead of *trespasses*."

Unless these traditions have honest Biblical significance, it would do us good to get rid of some of these itchy shirts and sweaty corduroys.

We might be out of season, but the experience could be refreshing!

"Naughty Smart or Good Smart?"

When Rose, our eldest daughter, was a little girl, she had a time deciding what people meant when they used the word smart. She would look up at me and ask, "Naughty smart or good smart?"

If we don't know a person's motives, or the circumstances, it is difficult to answer whether someone or something is "naughty smart or good smart." What appears "good smart," may in truth be "naughty smart."

We look at the advance in the field of science. Books that were science fiction a few years ago are now factual. Even with a staggering imagination, we cannot fathom the things that have been accomplished in these past few decades. We are certainly producing a smart generation!

Just a few minutes ago, I saw on television some pictures of the bombing of Hanoi. Fire was raging, people were salvaging their belongings, others were being carried out on litters—a ghastly scene!

Many intelligent minds planned the attack and saw it through. Those powerful bombs were the results of our great scientific research. A smart generation?

I seem to hear Rosie ask again, "Naughty smart or good smart?"

I'll Keep My Children

Friends of ours had a problem getting the right formula for their baby. We mentioned the fact that they might have to take the baby back to the hospital. Joe was listening and questioned, "Are they going to take the baby back and get another one?" There are moments of desperation when parents would feel like doing this.

The day Joe was down in the basement hammering spike nails into my potatoes, I would have liked to take him back and get another one, or the time the children decided to take inventory of our home library. I was sorry later that I scolded, because they were doing what Daddy did at his book store.

Even parents who dearly love their children find it pretty hard to say, "I love you," at three o'clock in the morning. Each child brings with him his own individual problems which the books don't tell about. He fits only into his own particular category. This is the reason that raising children is such a frustrating and interesting task. God planned it this way. He did not want us to be bored.

If all the children were sleeping in a row, and we could take our pick, not one of us would choose another child except his own.

CHRISTIANS

I don't have to be your brother at all.

"A Little Hot and a Little Cold"

It was getting chilly at our Sunday-school picnic, and I suggested to Libby that she put on her sweater. She refused the sweater by saying, "I want to be a little mixed up; a little hot and a little cold."

This is a typical human reaction. I like to be the happy-medium person, too: to my way of thinking, just right. I like to believe I'm progressive, but not radically so. Interested? Yes, but not involved. I try to appear friendly, when I can keep my distance. I want to be a Christian, without being fanatical.

However, when I think of the Apostle Paul, I cannot believe that he was "a little hot and a little cold." If Martin Luther had been a middle-of-the-roader, I doubt if those ninety-five theses would have been nailed to the church door.

We can be happy-medium and neutral, but what do we accomplish? We are like the Laodiceans of whom the Bible says: "I know you well—you are neither hot nor cold; I wish you were one or the other! But since you are merely luke-warm, I will spit you out of My mouth!" (REVELATION 3:15, 16, LIVING PROPHECIES).

This condemnation comes pretty close to home when we realize that being tepid Christians is worse than not being Christians at all.

From Gunman to Jesus

Joe was playing on the steps of our store, when one of the clerks came back from lunch. "I a gunman," he said. "Oh," she replied, "I don't think your Daddy would like that." He thought a minute and said, "Then I play Jesus."

There are many of us Christians who can turn our convictions off and on just that easily. If we think one crowd would like us one way, we cooperate. If we think another group would approve of something else, we do that. After all, we contend, when Paul was in Rome he did as the Romans did.

Our extremes may not go from gunman to Jesus, but we may appear just as ridiculous to the bystander who is watching the panorama of our Christian faith.

I have been guilty of agreeing with someone on a certain issue, and later, when another friend comes along with the opposite view, I nod my head again. I feel a twang of conscience, but I insist, "What else could I do?"

When I make a family law that I think is important, the children sometimes come back later with, "Everyone else is allowed to do it!" Against my better judgment, I change my mind and give in. The day before, I would have told anyone that the law was based on a deep-rooted conviction.

My Christian life is made up of many from-gunman-to-Jesus episodes.

"... One Blood All Nations ..."

"I'm getting sick of the way you're treating me," Joe told one of his sisters. "I don't have to be your brother at all."

Joe's reaction sounds so grown-up. It is the type of retaliation that resounds in our churches. It is prevalent in politics. It echoes throughout the United Nations. "I'm getting sick of the way you're treating me," is the theme of the labor unions. The whole adult world is saturated with this theory.

"I don't have to be your brother at all," we said at Hiroshima and Nagasaki. But the Lord told Cain, "... the voice of thy brother's blood crieth unto me from the ground" (GENESIS 4:10, KJV).

Who picks our brothers?

"God that made the world and all things therein . . . hath made of one blood all nations of men for to dwell on all the face of the earth, and hath determined the times before appointed, and the bounds of their habitation" (ACTS 17:24A, 26, KJV).

Did Christ demand a certain type of treatment? Did He claim any rights because of His position?

"He was oppressed, and he was afflicted, yet he opened not his mouth: he is brought as a lamb to the slaughter, and as a sheep before her shearers is dumb, so he openeth not his mouth" (ISAIAH 53:7, KJV).

I cannot choose nor disown my brothers, nor can I set a pattern as to how they should treat me.

In Christ, I see the example of how I must treat them.

"... I Can Go to Sleep"

One evening our whole family went, by chartered bus with a church group, to see the Phillies play the San Francisco Giants. It was my first major league game, and the Phillies did not help my enthusiasm.

It was late when we left for home. Joe was trying to get into a good sleeping position on the adjustable seat of the bus. He finally came and sat beside me, and went to sleep. Telling about it the next day, he said, "Whenever I get near Mommie, I can go to sleep."

In his pre-school days, a fuzzy blanket took care of his problems. Then his world became bigger, and Mother and Daddy were his refuge. He will be a man soon, and he will outgrow us.

Have we prepared him to face the fact that health and wealth do not offer absolute security? There are times when relatives and friends will let him down. Does he know an education alone will not bring security? There will be times when even his dog won't understand. He will need someone who is always there, and is interested in him. He will need someone who understands his characteristics, and his tendencies. He will need Christ!

"And Christ became a human being and lived here on earth among us and was full of loving forgiveness and truth" (JOHN 1:14, LIVING GOSPELS).

He will need God! If he can say, "In thee, O Lord, do I put my trust" (PSALMS 71:1, KJV), he will feel God near and will find rest.

"Glory to the New Born King!"

The first snow probably had something to do with Libby's statement, and also the fact that it was less than two weeks away from the exciting side of Christmas. "Every day, I can't stop singing, 'Glory to the new-born King'!" she exclaimed. God love her! What beautiful words to keep buzzing in your head! "Glory to the new-born King."

I get so busy sewing, decorating, baking, buying, wrapping, phoning, driving, mailing, and stamping, that no song has time to repeat itself in my head; so unless my activities "sing" this song, I lose the whole spirit of Christmas.

The Spirit of Christ is not revealed merely by the sending of scriptures-text greeting cards, nor by the displaying of a Nativity set. To keep Christ in Christmas, we must portray His characteristics.

Why has Santa Claus held such power through the years?

Because people become part of the act. They are the hands and feet of the benevolent Santa Claus. If Christians would use this same principle in trying to disclose the Spirit of Christ, we would see a different celebration.

I have often thought, "If I had never seen any Christmas decorations nor heard any Christmas legends, and I read the story of the first Christmas for the very first time—how would I start a celebration?" I should hope that I would start by singing, "Glory to the new-born King."

"I Got a Sad Feeling in Myself"

I quote Joe to describe my feelings. "I got a sad feeling in myself."

It was such a shock, the Sunday his family called and told us Jakie was gone! Twelve years old and he just slipped away from all of us. What they thought was just a common ailment of a few days, turned out to be a deadly disease.

Our families were the closest of friends. Their three "J's," Jim, Jake and Jon, and our one Joe, made quite a team. Jake had mischievous, dark eyes and an irresistible grin.

"He spoke to me when he was naughty and when he was nice," his mother remembers.

She recalled quite vividly an incident that happened one Sunday morning. While the children were getting ready for church, family tension filled the air, and the atmosphere was quite static. They finally arrived at church, took their seats, and began singing the beautiful hymns of the church; all except Jake. He gave his mouth that familiar twist of disgust, and glared at his mother 'til the tears rolled down her cheeks. His eyes seemed to burn the words, "You hypocrites."

A few weeks before he died, he wended his way in the

dark to his parents' bedroom. With his typical, vivid expressiveness, he said, "Now, I must become a Christian! If someone would hit me on my head and kill me, I would go to hell."

What a blessing for them to know that right in their bedroom that night, he found rest for his soul, and just a few weeks later, rest for his body, too.

But as his mother says, "His voice and his life ring on forever."

"Then I'll Know Who You Are!"

I was planning to attend Libby's Halloween parade at school. "What dress will you be wearing," she questioned. "I will be wearing my pink suit," I informed her. "Good," she exclaimed, "then I'll know who you are!"

It is quite possible that a stranger might identify me as the lady who wears the pink suit, but Libby should know me in any dress! She has known my physical features from the time she was a baby.

Couldn't she tell it was me the way I smile or wave my hand as she parades by? I know my six-year-old meant no offense and I was amused when she said it. However, it did raise some questions.

Do my neighbors and friends use my outward appearance as a means of identification? I would hardly convince you that we have a good doctor by telling you he always wears a white coat. The coat would be incidental. The doctor's qualifications are the important thing.

A Christian must manifest the fruits of the spirit. ". . . love, joy, peace, patience, kindness, goodness, faithfulness, Gentleness and self-control" (GALATIANS 6:22, 23, LIVING LETTERS); these characteristics must be woven into the way I treat my family, my neighbors, and the salesmen who call at the door.

The Bible says: "But if a person isn't loving and kind, it shows that he doesn't know God. For God is love" (1 JOHN 4:8, LIVING LETTERS).

People should detect that we are Christians by what we *are*, and not by what we *wear*.

"Love Two"

My husband was having our two-year-old son repeat a Bible verse after him. "Love one another," he said. "Love two," replied Joey.

He might have understood the verse as, "Love one and another." So he did some quick arithmetic and said, "Love two," or, at that young age, anything more than one is two, no matter how many. Better than memorizing, Joey grasped the truth of the verse.

Christ said these words, ". . . love one another . . ." and he continued, "as I have loved you . . ." (JOHN 13:34, KJV). This includes the smart alec you can't stand, plus the nosey neighbors.

There was one woman who made this verse extremely difficult for me. She was unkempt in every detail. I needed the truth of this verse just to sit near her. I dreaded to meet her when my babies were small. She loved children, and couldn't resist my clean, powdered babies. She would cuddle and coddle and I would wince and writhe. It was not easy to love her as Christ loved us, and I confess that I didn't accomplish it. Oh, I treated her civilly, but I didn't love her enough to demonstrate it.

Loving one another as Christ loves, includes the lovable and the unlovely, the irresistible and the repulsive. It means to "love two" or three, ten or twenty, enough to give our lives for them.

FRIENDS

I'll step real loud . . . .

They Are Gone

I felt sorry for Libby the day she said soberly, "Today was Becky's last day." Her little school friend, Becky, was moving, and maybe Libby would never see her again.

It would be interesting to know how many people we have met in one lifetime. Maybe we knew them for only a day, a week, or a year, and suddenly they are gone. Except by some remote chance, we will never see them again.

I wonder what happened to my school mate who gave me a used pencil for a gift, when I had scarlet fever in second grade?

In my childhood memories there is a man who suddenly turned up in a snow storm at the cellar door, and was invited to spend the night in our home. A perfect stranger to us! Many times, I have thought of the verse which says: "Don't forget to be kind to strangers, for some who have done this have entertained angels without realizing it" (HEBREWS 13:2, LIVING LETTERS)!

I remember the couple we met in a campground in Oregon, who loaned us their black frying pan to fry the fresh salmon we had caught.

Last summer, while camping in Ontario, Libby made friends with some children from Quebec, and within about two hours they pulled up stakes, and were gone.

Clerks, nurses, doctors, teachers, neighbors, classmates—people in all walks of life touch our lives, and then they are gone.

A sobering thought!

"What Was Life Like . . . ?"

With his voice sounding like a confirmed egotist, Joey asked, "What was life like before you got me?" We don't need to be too concerned about what life was like before we graced the scene, but what is it like now that we are here?

Our family knew a man we shall call Fred. Fred was left speechless by a cerebral hemorrhage. For the last ten years of his life, he could not talk, nor could he eat nor drink, unless he was lying flat on his back, and his wife put the nourishment in his mouth.

In those silent, frustrating years, when he was unable to communicate, there were times when tears would roll down his cheeks, and, with gestures, he would reach for heaven. There was an old friend of his who was a conductor on the evening train that made a stop at the local station.

For several years, Fred walked to the depot for that evening train, just to see his friend and sometimes to take him a little gift—a few shellbarks he had picked. Fred's mind didn't function as it once had, and his conductor friend understood. He accepted the nuts graciously, and assured Fred that he would eat them.

Fred's wife (now a widow) told me that when the weather was extremely bad, she would put a wrap on him and take him up on the top porch to see the train as it went over the underpass. The conductor would always be there to wave his daily greeting.

There are statesmen who influence many lives. There are authors, who win the Nobel Prize. There was a Christian conductor, who added meaning and unspoken joy to Fred's life, just by a short stop at the depot, or the wave of a hand from a puffing train. He deserves to hear Christ say, "When you did it to these My brothers you were doing it to Me!" (MATTHEW 25:40, LIVING GOSPELS).

If we have made an impression with our lives, not we, but others, will ask, "What was life like before you were here?"

"I'll Step Real Loud"

Remodeling sounds too dignified for a description of the way our kitchen looked: a blanket where a door should be, brick dust and termite eaten boards scattered all around.

My husband was trying to clean up some of this confusion with the help of our six-year-old son. They were carrying lumber across the street, and Daddy warned, "You must always take care, son, so you won't get hit. I need you yet." Joe thought for a moment, and then replied, "I'll step real loud and if you don't hear me you'll know I was hit," and he clopped away.

People need us. We need people. Some of us tiptoe through life so we will not be heard. We need to be conscious of each other. Sometimes, we need to "step real loud."

It was the evening before our trip to Philadelphia. We were taking our three-year-old to the Children's Hospital for observation. Our pediatrician wanted to make sure of his diagnosis. Having the baby sick, distresses the whole family.

Friends of ours, "stepped real loud" that night, and drove thirty miles just to spend the evening with us, to let us know they cared. They were neither relatives, nor neighbors. The husband was a salesman who called at our store. We needed them, and the awareness of their presence seemed to lighten the load.

Mansions and cottages, hospital beds and prison cells, apartment buildings and farm houses, are full of people who need to hear you "step real loud." It will help just knowing you are there.

"I Have So Many Friends"

We were in a situation where troubles seemed to come all at once; the type of predicament when you wonder, who are my friends?

Like Elijah, I sat under the juniper tree feeling sorry for myself.

We were in the living room, discussing this condition with a member of our church. Our small daughter was playing happily with her stuffed toys and dolls. The white (gray) cat, the wilted doll, and the shabby teddy bear, all mixed in with the better-looking toys, were lined up on the sofa. She was quite proud of her collection. Like someone who had just counted her blessings, she exclaimed, "I have so many friends."

An hour sermon could not have done for me what those five words did. It struck home immediately, and I knew it was meant for me. I had no reason to feel so discouraged and upset, when I could count my blessings.

Maybe you should hunt out your wilted dolls and shabby teddy bears (blessings you hadn't thought of for awhile). It will surprise you how good they feel. You will say, too, "I have so many friends."

"That Makes Me Famous!"

Joe is always looking for a way to identify himself with famous people.

If Mr. President were a cousin to the father of the fellow who married the daughter of his mother's ex-Sunday-school teacher, Joe would still declare, "That makes me famous!"

Collecting autographs of famous people is not my hobby. I have met a few celebrities in my time. I have seen a few more, at a distance. But they are all just people! They itch and scratch, sniffle and sneeze, laugh and cry, the same as you and I.

I've known a few important people in my time, who will not be found in *Who's Who* or a wax museum, for instance: the doctor who brought me into the world, and five years later wrestled with me on the floor, trying to convince me that a vaccination could be endured without novocaine; also my eighth grade teacher who discussed grown-up stuff with us at recess, making us feel very important; and the judges who were responsible for the only blue ribbon I ever won. It was in the first-grade singing contest.

No one needs to feel deprived, if he has not met the elite, or name-brand crowd. Everyday one can see nobility, and people of superior excellence.

Just this morning, I saw a crossing guard reach down and button a child's top button of her coat. The child looked up into the guard's face, with a look of admiration that is reserved for only special people and special events.

It is knowing people like this, that should make us feel grateful.

"You're My Third Friend"

One Mother's Day, Jenny wanted to say something nice to me. "Mother," she said, "you're my third friend; first God, then the Bible, and then you." Somehow, I didn't mind my rating. I felt she had paid me a rare compliment.

I wish I could keep things in their proper order, but this world is so distracting. Why can't I say, "Family, you're my third friend; first God, then the Bible, and then you."

Family life is demanding and necessary. My children should be well-clothed and fed. There have been times, though, when the task has completely enveloped me—diapers, bottles, thermometers, pills, dentist appointments, trips to the family doctor and the pediatrician, piano lessons, basketball practice, science fair projects. . . . I'm getting tired thinking about it.

Can I say, "Church you're my third friend?" My devotional life is more important than the coffee klatch, the home-makers' meeting, or choir practice. Do I say, "Neighbor, you're my third friend. I'll help you all I can, but my quiet time is more important than a cup of coffee"? I wish I could say, "World, you're my third friend."

The community I live in has a way of dictating to me how my lawn should look, or how my windows should be polished. The school which my children attend sets a pattern for dress, if I want to be "in."

How many migraines and neuroses could be avoided if we, like Jenny, could put the phases of life in their proper order!

"The Tears Did Roll Down"

The first day of kindergarten went fine for Joe. The second day he cried, because some other boy was scolded. The third day he told me he cried again, but to tell me he didn't cry long, he said, "The tears did roll down and there did be a smile."

That describes my feeling about my dear friend Ethel. We were shocked when we heard of her serious illness, and about six weeks later she died. So young! She was just forty-three years old. It was truly sad!

Ethel and I grew up in the same church. We double-dated many times. Our husbands were good friends from high-school days. Being a pastor's wife, her unselfishness was showered generously around the community. If a bed was needed by someone, their home was open. She was a mother to more than just her three sons—no matter what color or nationality.

What a blessing for the family to see her Christ-like spirit, radiating from that hospital bed! One evening she asked her husband for her robe and her slippers to take one last walk with him. He explained to her that she wasn't strong enough, but if at all possible they would take that walk later. She smiled contentedly. Ethel was like that. She never took that walk here on this earth.

Yes, the tears did roll down! I was sad—but glad I had the privilege of being her friend.

COMMUNICATING

When are we going to warm the house?

"When Are We Going To Warm the House?"

Children believe a thing just as they hear it. Nothing is symbolic or abstract to them. Because of this, children come to some unusual conclusions.

When Joe was three, I told him that Jesus lives in our hearts. He almost frightened me when he said, "I'm going to cut my tummy open to see Jesus."

I wish we could see the pictures that pass through children's minds when they misunderstand our grown-up talk.

We were attending a house warming for some friends, when Jenny piped up, "Mother, when are we going to warm the house?"

On one occasion I told Libby I was making a cherry pie for Washington's Birthday. "Are we going to give it to him?" she asked—a perfectly sensible question.

We often laugh when we think of the time my husband pulled up to a gas station and told the attendant, "Hi-test." Joe heard it and questioned, "Is his name Test?" Questions don't show a child's ignorance, but, rather, his intelligence.

Walter was talking about making a hotbed, which Joe did not understand. "If you get a hotbed," Joe asked excitedly, "can I sleep with you?"

Some children are adept at associating one thing with another, too. Libby had been at the YMCA swimming pool with her Daddy. She was demonstrating to me, with her arms, how the life guard was teaching them to swim. Then she said, "I didn't sing 'Running Over.'"

It must have been difficult for her to resist singing it, when she associated the arm movements with the motions of the little Sunday-school song, "Running Over."

To understand the expressions of a child, and to have a child understand you, is the most rewarding form of communication there is.

"... Name All My Dolls Susie"

Our four year old was trying to decide on names for her dolls. In her dilemma she said, "I'd like to name all my dolls Susie, (pause) but then I wouldn't know which one was Susie."

We have already made the mistake. The name Christian has become so widely used it now includes "atheistic Christianity." Theologians and laymen are in the middle, confused, concerned, and trying to decide which one is Christian. They advocate tolerance and acceptance, and try not to offend, but they still don't "know which one is Susie."

In the great surge of ecumenical movement, there are new areas where friendly chats become more difficult. The fundamentalists and the modernists, the liberals and the conservatives, are writing satirical books about each other. Communication is out of reach; dialogue is nonexistent; relating seems remote. They don't even speak the same language. The Tower of Babel couldn't have produced more confusion.

If Libby had made the mistake and named all her dolls Susie, I wonder how she would have remedied the situation?

Dimes for Calcutta

Libby's Sunday-school class was filling dime cards to help the needy in India. I have no way of knowing just what pictures are in Libby's mind about India, but every night Libby prays for the girls and boys in Calcutta.

When I give her fifty cents for her forty cent lunch, she wants to save the dime for Calcutta. Instead of a quarter for a pulled tooth, she asked for a dime to give for Calcutta. On our family shopping night, she saved her dime rather than take a ride on a mechanical space ship or jumping horse. Her teacher must have made a vivid impression on her mind as to the need in India.

I know the needs of India too. One of my childhood friends is a missionary in India. She translates literature into the native language. I've seen her waving from the deck as her ship pulled out of the New York harbor. I visited her when she was home on furlough and gave her some tithe money. She spoke and sang on our radio program some years ago. I have more connection with India than Libby and yet Calcutta is not very real to me.

Has my sympathy for mankind become distracted by my own selfish wants?

If we are ever to communicate with people, it must be in the spirit of love. To love is to care. Dimes for Calcutta is caring.

"... A Chimney Without a House"

Our small artist was drawing pictures. What she lacked in talent, she made up in creativeness.

One day she drew a rectangle that was standing on end. She looked at it with pride and said, "This is a chimney without a house." I would never have guessed, if she hadn't told me.

I was rather dubious that Libby meant to make a chimney. I think that look on her face, which I thought was pride, was really surprise. It's a lot safer to name your picture after it's done. Maybe there could be a house without a chimney, but a chimney without a house doesn't make sense.

We live in an age that encourages creative thinking, creative art, and creative writing. New activities in the church and school encourage self-expression. Think for yourself, is the trend. Experiment with life. Throw this together and that together, and see what you come up with. Be daring; be reckless. Even though it doesn't make sense to anyone else, it is your own creation.

If I can't paint a picture the others enjoy, if I can't make a speech that most people understand, if I can't write this book so that it touches your heart, I'm wasting my time.

I might as well be drawing "chimneys without houses."

"I Know Why You Parked Down Here"

I have two locations where I pick up Libby, after school. In bad weather I meet her in the semi-circular driveway, directly in front of the school. On fair weather days, I park near the shallow lake which is next to the playground. On the first snowy afternoon of the season, I thought, "I'll park near the lake; that will give her more time to walk through the snow."

She was all smiles as she walked toward the car. After she was settled on the seat, she said, "I know why you parked down here; you wanted me to have some fun." I never cease to marvel at a child's intuition. That is exactly what I had in mind!

It is next to impossible to hide your feelings from children. They read your eyes, gestures, smiles, frowns, posture and gait. Long before they add two plus two numerically, they can figure out adults.

They consider your personality, plus your actions, and inevitably give the right answer. No stone is left unturned in a child's extensive probing. "I just knew it," or, "I just guessed it," are familiar phrases which mean, "I psychoanalyzed you and this is what I came up with."

In a child's mind, even where you park your car can shed new light on you.

"I'll Get Up When I Want To"

"I'll get up when I want to," declared our three year old from her bed.

The revolutionary concept of freedom did not originate on the college campus. The idea of doing what you want to do, and wearing what you want to wear, has its beginning inside the receiving blanket.

The college crowd of today were the children of yesterday. They grew up during a period when magazine articles and books proclaimed that children must express themselves. To restrict their impulses could impair them for life.

As a result, we have many working for college degrees who have never received their nursery diplomas. They are grown people with tantrums, insisting that they will wear what they want to wear, when they want to wear it. They will not be prisoners of conformity.

To be able to be your unrestrained self is living life in the raw. The young people insist on honesty and reality. It is a way to escape the dull and meaningless routine of the conformist.

As parents of this younger generation, we can hardly expect

to reap something different from what we have sown. We have allowed our children to display their feelings and have not tried to stop them. Their screaming and kicking on the floor, which we were told to ignore, have now developed into protest marches and sit-ins.

The result of this experiment should be conclusive: the Bible method of child training is still on top.

"Foolishness is bound in the heart of a child; but the rod of correction shall drive it far from him" (PROVERBS 22:15, KJV).

"I'll get up when I want to," must be dealt with in the crib.

"Give Me That Old Television"

It took a long time for us to decide about getting a television for our family. Now that we have it, I'm not sure we made the right decision.

Joe, of course, was pulling for it for a long time. When he was quite small, we went to see the film *A Man Called Peter*. In the picture, they sang the song "Give Me That Old Time Religion."

Sometime later, he was trying to tell me something about the film. "You know," he explained, "when they sang, 'Give Me That Old Television.'" The closing phrase "and it's good enough for me," described his feelings I'm sure, because at that point, any old television would do.

I am concerned about the influence this intruder will have on our children. I know trial and error is the only way of testing something, but these are our children, and they go through their formative years only once.

Some of the most convincing and attractive commercials on television are those produced by the liquor and tobacco industries. These commercials are especially disturbing to me.

Every few minutes, one can see how sparkling wine, and the "just right" beer, can brighten a day. Why, I ask, must sports events be sponsored almost entirely by products the athlete should not use?

All these years, we have tried to instill decency into our children. We can watch one TV program and realize that every basic principle we taught has been challenged.

Television is here to stay; it becomes a way of life. I try to justify myself by thinking my children must learn to live with it. The tremendous impact that television makes on our homes, however, makes me wonder if Joe should have sung, "Give me that old television," a little while longer.

Questions and Answers

Joe was looking in the mirror at the vacant spot where a tooth should have been. "How do they put a tooth in there?" he asked. "It just grows in," I answered. "Do they put a seed in?" he persisted.

When I think back to the many questions I have answered, some carefully, others carelessly, I wonder if the answers were right.

Did I create an interest in God when Libby asked, "How did God make hisself?" I remember the time Rosie inquired, "Mother, why wasn't Jesus married?" Taken aback, I said, "Well, he wasn't like us." Coming to my rescue, Rosie continued, "In a way, it would have been sort of a mixed marriage!"

The responsibility of being the parents of five children, answering their questions and giving the right answers, is hitting home to me more everyday.

I realize that we are involved too often in providing their physical needs and we forget it is their souls that live on.

As each cuddly bundle was placed in my arms, I did not realize the gigantic task that we parents have. It is not just helping our children safely through childhood, but fortifying them for life.

What they learned, or did not learn, from us, will affect our grandchildren and their children.

PRAYER

. . . but I don't know what to worry about.

Conversational Prayer

The one big thrill that parents are allowed is to hear their children pray for each other. They can be arguing all day, but when you hear their sincere prayers for each other at night, you know everything is all right.

Joe knew Jenny was worried about her lessons again. That night he prayed, "Dear Lord, we pray that Jenny won't get so hepped up about her school work."

It's not new for children to use conversational prayer. To a child, prayer is as natural as breathing. What a treat it must be for God to hear these little prayers that flow right from their hearts!

I can remember that as a child, I prayed without ceasing for my mother who had a growth, which we thought might be a tumor. To this day, I have a feeling it might have been one. I breathed prayer; I walked praying, I played praying, and the growth did disappear.

I don't believe in practicing conversational prayer as one would practice a piano lesson. Rehearsed conversational prayer can be just as meaningless and routine as a prayer that is prayed with *thee's*, *thou's*, *thy's* and *thine's*. It can soon become small talk, and sound like you are trying to make conversation.

It was years ago that James Mongomery wrote the hymn:

> Prayer is the soul's sincere desire,
> Unuttered or expressed,
> The motion of a hidden fire
> That trembles in the breast.
>
> Prayer is the simplest form of speech
> That infant lips can try;
> Prayer the sublimest strains that reach
> The Majesty on high.

Worry About Not Worrying

The worry bug of our family said one day, "Mother, I just think I got to worry about something, but I don't know what to worry about."

Did you ever worry that you were not worrying? I was well acquainted with this feeling, but it startled me that a child was bothered by it.

Some of us have so conditioned ourselves to worry that it baffles us when we stop. It's like being in a room when a motor stops. The silence becomes embarrassing. No one knows what to say. We had gotten so used to the motor noise in the background, we seemed to need it as an accompaniment.

Worry is the most exhausting and senseless thing I do. Why do I want to keep on? It is just like any other sin; we don't want to give it up. We feel some sort of security in just hearing the motor run.

It is a sad commentary on our Christian life, if we become addicted to chain worrying. Before someone organizes Worriers Anonymous, I've learned there is an easier way. "Let Him have all your worries and cares, for He is always thinking about you and watching everything that concerns you" (I PETER 5:7, LIVING LETTERS).

Dead End or New End

The city of Bethlehem, Pennsylvania, is an exciting place during the Christmas season. In the Central Moravian Church is the well-known Christmas *Putz* (crèche). In this church, the traditional candle-light services are held. Going to Bethlehem to see the lights is part of the Christmas celebration in our area. Overlooking all this festivity, high on the mountain, is the star of Bethlehem.

One night, our family tried to find the road that led to the star. It was not our first attempt. I remember, quite vividly, hunting the same road in our courtship days, without success. This night, too, we were unsuccessful. Every road ended with a *Dead End* sign. We were almost ready to give up, when Joey (eager to get to the star) persisted, "We'll find a *New End* soon."

And we did! We had been going toward the star from the wrong direction. The narrow gravel road approaches the star from the opposite side. It was Joe's urging that helped us to keep trying.

A *Dead End* sign means only that we cannot go further on that road. Sometimes we lose heart and don't have the energy or the desire to keep plugging: then a *Dead End* means *The End*. It is our responsibility to give encouragement to such frustrated souls.

The Bible instructs us: "Share each other's troubles and problems, and so obey our Lord's command" (GALATIANS 6:2, LIVING LETTERS).

During a *Dead End* experience, our family received unsolicited direction and encouragement from thousands of miles away. A note reached us, with the information that the prayer group of a publishing house in California was remembering us in prayer.

With this kind of support, we couldn't help but "find a *New End* soon."

Play It Fair

Jenny and Joe were discussing the value of prayer before exams. Joe, being the logical soul that he is, remarked, "I always try to remember to pray before a test. I pray that the Lord will help me remember the stuff I studied. You can't expect God to help you remember the stuff you didn't study."

Fair play is important in any game. If we understand the rules of the game, we should not be shocked when a penalty is called against us.

Many of us do not play it fair with God. Joe is right! "You can't expect God to help you remember the stuff you didn't study." God is not obligated to answer prayers that will promote our laziness. The Bible says, "And when you do ask you don't get it because your whole aim is wrong—you want only what will give *you* pleasure" (JAMES 4:3, LIVING LETTERS).

To pray for the salvation of others, so life will be more pleasant for us, is a selfish prayer with the wrong aim. I have heard of pastors who are so busy with the Lord's work that they have turned their children over to the Lord to raise. They insist the Lord is more capable to do the job than they are. When you plant a garden, do you say, "Lord now keep the weeds out. It's so much easier for you to do it than I"? To play it fair, we must accept our share of the responsibility.

"You can't expect God to help you remember the stuff you didn't study."

"And Boy! Help 'Em Learn About Jesus!"

Children pray so honestly—so down to earth—that sometimes it's hard for me to keep a sober face. There have been times in our family worship when the whole family could not resist laughing, because the prayer of a younger child was so blunt and unpretentious. I suppose this could have a damaging effect on the smaller child, but I haven't worried too much about it. Children can sense whether you are enjoying them or making fun of them.

One night Joey was praying for children who didn't have food and clothing. Probably realizing that food and clothing were not enough, he continued earnestly, "And Boy! help 'em learn about Jesus!"

With all our interest in cleaning up the ghettos, and with our colleges producing social workers by the score, crime is increasing at a tremendous rate, even in our renewal areas. People cannot be made good by a new sweater or an extra sandwich. However, it will help to make them more comfortable. Unless they have changed their motives and desires, however, the extra calories will only renew their strength for returning to more atrocious deeds than before.

We have Biblical support for supplying the physical needs of the world, but we are not meeting the total daily requirement if we do not relieve the spiritual malnutrition as well.

EXCUSES

This ribbon hates me.

"See, I Cut the Price Off"

Joe was cutting a magazine which he knew should not be cut. When I surprised him and he sensed my disapproval, he quickly said, "See, I cut the price off."

He knew that this excuse could sound legitimate, but being his mother, I could see through him.

We don't need to shake our heads and wonder, "How do they learn these tricks?" Start keeping track of all the excuses you make in a day. Excuses very seldom tell the whole truth; just enough truth to make it sound right when you say it.

Later that day, I excused myself out of a job—really I did. A pastor called and asked me to conduct a workshop on ways of teaching music to primary children. I told him, "First of all, my knowledge of music is very elementary." Which it is! "Most of my teaching experience has been with older pupils." Which it has! I think I got it across to him that I would be like a fish out of water. Which I would!

He made a remark, and I wasn't sure what he meant. It was something to the effect that he wouldn't want me to go out of my way and spend a lot of time digging up information that wasn't in my field. He was so polite and understanding, though. . . .

I didn't mean to imply, before I got the phone call, that all excuses are phony. What I was trying to say is that too many of our excuses sound like Joe, when he said, "See, I cut the price off." They sound logical, but they do not give quite the whole story.

" *This Ribbon Hates Me*"

The baby of our family was having trouble with her hair ribbon not staying tied. She finally became so upset she declared, "This ribbon hates me."

I smiled. The hair ribbon couldn't do anything good or bad. Why would she blame a ribbon? For the same reason we blame people and things that have nothing to do with our problems. Somehow, it seems to put us in the clear.

I may run smack into a door. Instantly, I'm blaming the fellow who closed the door. I touch wet paint and look at the sign. "One sign isn't enough," I mutter. "Besides, why don't they make the sign bigger?" I open a box of corn flakes with a jerk and it flies all over the place. "Stupid boxes," I blurt. "With all the brains available to reach outer space, you'd think they could make a decent cereal box."

From Adam and Eve on down, this is what we all contend with. We are always looking for someone or something to blame. It is one of the first characteristics to manifest itself in a child, and a hard one to deal with through life.

Natural Curve Toward Sin

My husband was singing the hymn, "I Love to Steal Awhile Away."

Joey was listening and remarked, "OK, I'm going to steal something too."

Our human nature has a natural curve toward sin.

Paul says, "So you see how it is: My new life tells me to do right, but the old nature that is still inside me loves to sin. Oh, what a terrible thing this is!" (ROMANS 7:24, LIVING LETTERS).

Recently in our city, a carpenter, who was working on a renovation project in an empty building, found 5,699 dollars. The old money was stuffed in a cigar box and a candy tin, under old newspapers dating back to 1924.

The man said he wrestled with his conscience for about an hour, before turning in the money at the newspaper office. "It was like the devil was pulling on one arm and an angel pulling on the other," he claimed. "I feel good now," he continued. "I have a good conscience. It's like after going to confession—like a new-born baby." I was amazed, however, to hear the remarks about this carpenter. Some felt he should have kept it. "If nobody knew it was there, nobody would have missed it."

I heard one man on a call-in show on the radio say that if his child had found it, he would have had to tell him to turn it in, because of trying to teach him right. But if he (himself) had found it, he would have kept it and not felt guilty.

The Apostle Paul continued: "Who will free me from my slavery to this deadly lower nature?" (ROMANS 7:25, LIVING LETTERS).

"Thank God! It has been done through Jesus Christ our Lord. He has set me free" (*Ibid*).

Honest Questions

One day when Joe was just a little fellow, he was telling me the story of *The Three Bears*. When he came to the place where the bears decided to go for a walk, his face suddenly went blank. He continued the story, however, and when Goldilocks made her appearance, Joe looked at me with suspense and asked dramatically, "And guess what her name was?"

I know questions make story telling interesting, but this question was used as a bluff. Joe had forgotten the name of Goldilocks!

Many questions are asked to camouflage the truth. "But today," it is said, "we ask honest questions."

Who am I? How can I be truly honest with myself? Why do I do the things I do?

Thus we pick ourselves apart, into microscopic pieces. It makes a provocative display. The real problem comes when we try to assemble the puzzle. There's always that piece missing!

Do we ask these honest questions because it is the socially accepted way of self-analysis? The Bible gives us the harsh truth! The Bible does not bluff or pretend. We read, "The heart is deceitful above all things, and desperately wicked: who can know it?" (JEREMIAH 17:9, KJV). It's just that simple!

There is no socially acceptable way of saying it. Unless we are willing to admit this basic truth, our honest questions are merely used as scapegoats for something we don't want to face.

A Qualified Candidate

I was crabby, irritable, and just plain hard to live with. Joe, being affected by my mood, suggested, "Boy, Mom, you could do a whole bunch of aspirin commercials tonight."

Most of us demand too much of ourselves, physically and mentally. Our daily schedules could use two of us.

I read recently that it is possible for certain types of noises to cause depression. In our home there are endless noises. We hear the washer, dryer, refrigerator, freezer, two air conditioners, one dehumidifier, the oil burner, two exhaust fans, the television, four radios, and two record players. There are two door bells, two telephones, and one piano—not forgetting the rumpus and vibration that is caused by a family of seven.

Jenny, our studious senior, has learned that the place to escape from all this racket is under the hood of her hair dryer. In her desperation to study, she combats noise with more noise.

It's not just the noise in our houses, but the sounds outside, too: the rumbling of cars, the screeching of brakes, and the zooming of jets. Horns, sirens, and whistles are all part of this noisy serenade.

I'm not sure that these noises produce the pulsations causing tenseness and depression, but I need some excuse for my moods.

It isn't exactly a compliment to be a qualified candidate for "a whole bunch of aspirin commercials."

There Must Be a Reason

Becky loved coffee from the time she was a little girl. I tried to tell her it wasn't good for her, but the argument "you won't grow big if you drink coffee," could not be proved. Jenny loved milk and was always tiny; Becky was bigger and stronger and was fond of coffee.

When Joey was three years old, I took him with me to visit a semi-invalid mother and daughter. Sizing up the situation, he must have thought there was some good reason why these ladies were sick. Right there in front of them, he admonished, "You shouldn't drink so much coffee!" Evidently my dissertation on drinking coffee was getting through to Joe instead of Becky; however, his application to this circumstance was rather embarrassing for me.

This incident reminds me of an experience we had when

epilepsy struck a member of our family. Seizures were so frequent, we lived through a nightmare for a year and a half. People were concerned, and many prayed. Only parents in similar circumstances know the questions we asked ourselves, searching for answers where there were no answers.

One well-meaning friend—thinking, too, that there must be a reason—wrote us a letter with her explanation. Being against instrumental music, this dear soul thought possibly the reason for the illness was that my husband sold recordings of organ music.

Seeking explanations was also prevalent in Christ's day. " 'Master,' His disciples asked Him, 'Why was this man born blind? Was it a result of his own sins or those of his parents?' " (JOHN 9:2, LIVING GOSPELS). And then comes the balm for us anxious, questing parents. " 'Neither,' Jesus answered. 'But to demonstrate the power of God' " (v. 3).

FAITH

And I thought you were my buddy!

We Have Too Much

"What do you want for Christmas?" Joe asked Libby. "Toys," she replied. "But I have so many," she continued, "I don't know which ones I don't have."

Isn't it true, we have too much—America has too much? Instead of teaching our children to share, we buy a bicycle for each one. We want to save ourselves the argument, and the trouble of deciding whose turn it is.

I was in a children's shop, and I overheard a clerk telling a customer, "I don't take any pay; I take it all out in clothes for Sallie. Of course, Sallie has more clothes than she needs." I'm presuming it was a part-time job. Do mothers work to spring the hinges on the toy closet and acquire enough clothes for Sallie to be twins?

Our teen-age girls feel sorry for Libby's age, with its talking dolls and burping dolls, dolls that frown and smile, and dolls that cry wet tears. Jenny and Becky seem to think that creating these effects oneself was more fun.

In a day that preaches creativity from all angles, there seems to be less and less to create. Everything is done for us. Even cake mixes are too much trouble. We have so much, but we want more, more, more.

Did you ever wonder how to teach your children about faith, when the Bible says, "Now faith is the substance of things hoped for, the evidence of things not seen" (HEBREWS 11:1, KJV)?

What do we need to trust God for? Not our food—our freezers are full. Not warm beds—our electric blankets take care of that. Let's hope and pray that these children who say, "I have so many toys, I don't know which ones I don't have," will not grow up to be a faithless generation.

Neutrons, Protons, Electrons, and God

Her sisters stood by aghast as six-year-old Libby rattled off the parts of an atom: "Neutrons, protons and electrons!" Whereupon, she proceeded to explain her new coloring book from school called "Professor Atom." In her slow, choppy, first-grade style, she read, "Thirty-six billion-billion atoms could go on the head of a pin."

"Poor Libby," I thought, "don't tell me she will go through first grade without hearing the story of *The Little Red Hen!*"

Much of this information about Professor Atom was new to me too, so I turned to the glossary in the back of the book. The following words were defined: Atomic Nuclear Reactor, Geiger Counter, Nucleus, Radiotherapy, Albert Einstein, Madam Curie, and Fission.

There were pictures showing how a reactor affects the turbine, and the turbine the generator. According to this first grade coloring book: "Everything in the world is made up of atoms. They are so tiny that you cannot see them. Atomic energy is the power that is released from splitting atoms."

I could respond to this information by saying, "I don't believe it, because no one has ever seen an atom." However, I must believe there is such a thing as an atom, the same as I have no alternative but to believe there is a God.

I simply cannot deny the power of either.

"Button My Jacket for Gemini Nine"

One morning Libby requested, "Will you button my jacket for Gemini Nine?"

What a colorful way of asking to have her dress buttoned! More than that, it brought results; she got through to me on the first try. Sometimes it takes the spectacular to awaken me from my absentmindedness, or as Libby will sometimes exclaim in her frustration, "Mother, are you out of your mind?"

It seems that the only way to attract attention in this competitive world is to do or say something so shocking that it makes people stop dead in their tracks. The things that are said might be ridiculous, but maybe the comments were brought on by our being inattentive and unconcerned.

Statements are being made in the religious world today that are awakening even the spiritually dead. People who couldn't have cared less if God were dead or alive now suddenly rise in defense of a living God. I don't know if this is what the theologians had in mind when they propagated the God is dead theory, but as a friend says, "God is so imaginative." God must work with what's available, and He is demonstrating that He can use a news release of His death as a bulletin of His very existence.

These shockers can sober us, and make us conscious of our responsibility. Maybe it takes, "Button my jacket for Gemini Nine," to put us in action.

"It's Part of Life"

One summer day, Jenny was fussing and griping about her mosquito bites. Mosquito bites aren't exactly fun, but neither do I class them as tragedy. I finally got so tired of hearing her groaning that I exclaimed, "It's part of life, and you' gotta take it."

I didn't realize it made such an impression on her, until she started using my exact words on others. It was hard to get sympathy at our house for quite some time. "It's part of life, and you' gotta take it," became a family slogan.

We are not exempt from mosquito bites, measles, or Asian flu because we are Christians or live good lives. They are the price we pay for being part of this flesh and blood world.

Job said, "Man that is born of a woman is of few days, and full of trouble" (14:1, KJV). The Bible says he was upright and feared God, yet Job had a catalog of afflictions like few of us will ever endure.

Whatever this world has to offer in the department of trouble, Christians must expect it, too.

Christian parents watch their children suffer through long, anxious nights. Their children burn with fever or choke on pretzels, too.

In our hospital wards, saints and sinners meet on common ground. God can use these experiences to mature us, to help us understand the feelings of others. He does not promise always to help us out of trouble.

We read, "God is our refuge and strength, a very present help in trouble" (PSALMS 46:1, KJV).

Even though it's part of life, God helps us take it.

"And I Thought You Were My Buddy!"

We were visiting another church, and our young clown was putting on quite a show. After the service, my husband gave him a lecture in rather certain terms and told him it was getting past the funny stage. Joe sat and listened, then grumbled, "And I thought you were my buddy!"

The parent-child relationship so often reflects our relationship with God.

I make plan after plan. I make a dental appointment for Monday, a hairdressing appointment for Tuesday. Wednesday

I race around, to and fro, from place to place. Thursday night I show slides to the Golden Age Club. Friday is just like the other days. Saturday, I wind up with all my cleaning, baking, and one grand headache, plus my Sunday-school lesson to study. I am tense, edgy, and completely exhausted. Somewhere I feel God has let me down. Christians shouldn't have nerve trouble, I muse.

You are late for a speaking engagement. You leap into your car, and of all things, the gas gauge registers near empty. So you decide to get gas on the way home. Within three miles of your destination, the jalopy starts the hiccoughs. "Oh, no Lord," you cry, "You can't let this happen to me now."

We create our own distressing situations; we get ourselves in jams. How can we have the nerve to say to God, "And I thought You were my buddy"?

TODAY

...she sure inherited a big gene there.

"... The Nicest Bed in the World"

"I have the nicest bed in the world," announced our son contentedly.

The second-hand iron bed and spring cradled the bargain priced mattress. As Shakespeare said, "There is occasions and causes why and wherefore in all things" (*Henry V*, Act 5, Scene 1).

The occasion was laundry day. The cause of this dramatic statement was the smell and feel of clean, fresh, air-dried sheets.

Contentment is hard to find these days. When I come home from a friend's new house, my house looks drab. I need new lined drapes and the flamingo pink walls look sickening. The man of the house has car fever: after visiting the new car lot, our old car has suddenly taken a turn for the worse.

So one hangs the new drapes and the driveway sports a brand-new model; now another room needs redecorating or a speed boat hitch is added to the car.

Discontentment will work in you like cancer. Early detection is necessary for a cure. When you feel it coming on, go wash your sheets and hang them in the fresh air to dry. It is just the touch of luxury you need to say contentedly, "I have the nicest bed in the world."

A word of warning: don't start wishing you had clean sheets every night or you are right back where you started from.

Take Off Your Coats and Sit Down

"Are we going to take off our coats and sit down?" This was Joey's way of asking if we were going to stay for awhile.

Today there are too many people who do not have time to take off their coats and sit down. We don't allow ourselves time to visit old friends, to exchange our problems, and to encourage each other.

Many of us are too busy and seem to be unable to control it. Did anyone have a gun in your back when you promised to serve on that church committee, or to be president of PTA? The pace at which we live is so frantic that even in our own homes we hardly have time to take off our coats and sit down. Being active in worthwhile things sometimes leaves our children neglected as much as children whose parents frequent the saloons. The results often bear a striking resemblance.

Where will we find the answer? Must we go on living dizzily from day to day like an accelerated movie?

You will not find the solution, if you stand at the door with your hand on the knob. That meeting tonight is not a matter of life or death. So come in, take off your coat and sit down!

Heredity or Environment

Referring to an action of his sister, Jenny, Joe said, "Boy, she sure inherited a big gene there." It was not a commendable gene, I might add.

The battle still goes on—is it heredity or environment?

Both my husband and I are procrastinators, yet we have a child who is highly disciplined. Jenny not only makes deadlines on time, but has the project completed long before it is due.

She lays her school things out at night, to save confusion in the morning. She makes notes to herself about the things she should remember. She gets up in plenty of time, so she doesn't have to rush. She is so organized, it is frustrating. Nothing of my unscheduled, unorganized routine, has ever rubbed off on Jenny.

Her sister is directly opposite. As Rosie sometimes says, "When I sneeze, everything gets out of place." This could be blamed on her environment. I like a spotlessly clean house too, but I don't have what it takes to keep it that way (which incidentally is no fault of my home environment).

I was raised in a home where we didn't just dust the furniture, we chamoised it. Not even towels and wash cloths were put away without being ironed. Socks and shoe strings were the only apparel we didn't iron.

If someone should be able to trace my problem to my genes, what could I do about my heredity? If it's from my childhood environment, how could I change that? By the time the specialists have it figured out, the kaleidoscope moves, and a whole new design appears.

Isolation Ward or Primitive Area

Joe was having a bout with three-day measles, with symptoms of appendicitis as well. I tried to explain to him that if he had to go to the hospital, he would have to be in the isolation ward. When Jenny came home from school that afternoon, he explained to her, "If I have to go to the hospital, I will have to go in the primitive area."

Since our family is more familiar with camp grounds, than we are with hospitals, I suppose it was only natural for him to make this mistake, especially since there is a similarity. Seclusion, solitude, and privacy are the characteristics of both places. These features, that make the isolation ward undesirable, are the main attraction to the camper in the primitive area.

There are days when I'd love to be secluded and unvisited, but to have loneliness forced upon me, or to have no choice about being anti-social: this is another matter. So much of life, however, is not what we prefer. It is, therefore, important that we find enjoyment in the undesirable situations, too.

Maybe you need rest and quietness, but to find it in a sick bed is not what you have in mind.

When a doctor gives us medicine, dare we argue about the kind of bottle it comes in? We cannot quarrel whether what we need comes via a rest in the hospital or a vacation in the wilderness.

"Have a Good Day, Mommie"

First grade is not what it used to be. I should know, because our fifth child is in it.

There are endless details to worry about: envelopes for the United Fund, envelopes for school insurance, slips to sign for field trips, or physical and dental examinations. Some days Libby brings home more "mail" than the mailman leaves in our box.

This year there is a new problem. The cafeteria offers a choice of food. You can get the type "A" lunch which costs forty cents, or the snack-plate special for twenty-five. However, with the snack plate, you must buy your milk extra, and your dessert too, if you want it. So bringing forty cents does not necessarily mean you want the type "A" lunch. It is not only bewildering to Libby, but to her mother as well, and my heart goes out to the first-grade teachers.

One September morning, while Libby was still in the adjusting period, I drove her to school as usual. She stepped from the car and, as though she had an afterthought, turned and said brightly, "Have a good day, Mommie; don't worry about me."

Well! She looked so confident that I could not help but take her advice. Isn't it amazing how a few well-chosen words can have the effect of a tranquilizer?

A Dream in Each Eye

There is always competition in a family of seven. It might be either to see who can eat the most or who had the wildest dream. Our Libby Lou stopped us all one morning when she announced, "I had two dreams at one time, one in one eye and one in the other eye." Bless her heart! Many, these days, don't have a dream in any eye.

I scrutinize closely when a young person knows exactly what he has in mind for a career: it is so rare. Our young people sometimes graduate from college with no desire to work in the field of their major. They head into graduate work to see if they can find themselves. The ink is hardly dry on their diplomas when they leave for exchange posts in Europe, still afraid to strike out on their own. Why? Youth should be full of visions and dreams.

We've given our children educational toys and denied them the privilege of inventing. We give them television that requires only that they sit (or lie) and watch. We give them sports cars for birthday gifts with promises of bigger things for Christmas. What is left to dream about? The vague dreams they might have regarding their futures are squelched by aptitude tests.

It is not necessary to have a dream in each eye, but the Bible says, "Where there is no vision, the people perish . . ." (PROVERBS 29:18 KJV).

Things I Cannot Change

Everyday looked shiny and new to Libby. There was one thing that could tarnish her day, however, and that was the appearance of a dog.

It was a day like this when she declared, "I wish God would tie doggie up." She didn't realize that there might be another dog around the corner, and another still farther on. She was too young to understand that God does not take all "dogs" out of our lives.

A real master of dogs will tell you, "Of all things, don't run. Look the dog straight in the eye and don't act scared." I had one encounter with a dog named Bullets. He didn't give me a chance to look him square in the eye, and I didn't have time to ask God to tie him up. He sneaked up behind me and sank his canine tooth right into my ankle.

There are some unpleasant experiences in life for which no amount of preparation could spare us. They creep up on us quietly, without so much as a rustle.

If Libby grows up to be like her sister Jenny, she will never like dogs. This doesn't alter the fact that dogs are here to stay and she might as well accept them.

> God grant me the serenity to accept the things
>   I cannot change,
> The courage to change the things I can,
> And the wisdom to know the difference.

High Numbers

"I'm not playing," Libby fumed, when Joe asked her to play *Uncle Wiggly*.

So Joe proceeded to draw a card for her which said, "Ten hops." Libby rudely grabbed the card away from Joe. "I thought you weren't playing," he said. "I'm only playing when I get high numbers," she retorted.

You can't play a game like that, and you can't play life like that, either. If the card says you go to the Bow-wow Dog House, according to the rules of *Uncle Wiggly*—you go.

There are some people who always seem to pick high numbers. Everything seems to go their way. For them, life just seems to click. They go merrily along, planning, building, working, banking, buying, and bragging, with little thought to the possibilities of interruptions.

I keep thinking—somewhere in that pile is a card which says:

> Please don't say it's very hard
> But you must now draw one red card.

If *Uncle Wiggly* has gained any ground up to this point, a red card could spell disaster. As a Christian, however, I must be careful that this thinking does not turn to jealousy, that I do not wish misfortune on others.

To say we will play only if we get high numbers would mean that for most of life we would be quitters. High or low numbers, our only hope of ever winning is to keep playing the game.

TOMORROW

This isn't God's Book. It's mine.

Heaven

We have taught our children that there is no night in heaven, that God never sleeps, and that he always hears us when we pray. Thinking about heaven, Libby stated, "When you die you get alive again in heaven. That would be neat if you could take your TV along and stay up all night."

When Joe was small he commented, "Jesus stays up all night and all day. Him lucky!" My niece asked her mother one day, "Mother, will I have to take naps in heaven? If not, I hope I die today." The promise of no night there is what makes heaven a heaven, to most children. Children talk freely of heaven; they wonder about heaven. One day Libby asked, "Does Jesus have his own church?"

I overheard Joey telling his friend, Bobby, "We saw Jesus, say we did, when he was finished making us." I don't know what Bobby said, but I have a feeling he agreed. Modern theology, thank goodness, had not yet confused them. Since heaven is such a desirable place, it is not uncommon to hear a child express his desire to go there. Mothers and fathers begin to worry when a child talks about going to heaven. I know; I've worried about this many times. When Joe was four, he said, "I'm ready to go to heaven, and if Jesus picks me up I'm going to sit on His lap." Such simple faith! And according to the Bible, we must possess it too.

"About that time the disciples came to Jesus to ask which of them would be greatest in the Kingdom of Heaven! Jesus called a small child over to Him and set the little fellow down among them. And said, 'Truly, except you turn to God from your sin and become as little children, you will never even get into the Kingdom of Heaven'" (MATTHEW 18:1-3 LIVING GOSPELS).

"It's a Good Tired"

The effects of a childhood disease lasted many months with Joe. He was extremely tired and was left sluggish and languid; as he described it, "sick tired." Even normally healthy people become tired, as Joe found out again, but this he explained: "It's a good tired."

To lie in bed and be the victim of either *sick tired* or *good tired* is the difference between night and day. When it's sick tired, you ache and pain, throb and toss. The right spot in the bed cannot be found. Even breathing seems too much trouble. Though overly tired, there is no rest.

When you can say, "It's a good tired," your symptoms are different. You ache, but you don't pain. You can find rest, without a bed. You can breathe deeply and enjoy the benefits. It is a *good tired* because you know that you have worked and things have been accomplished. You sense the feeling of worth, which we all must feel—like an exhausted mother after she gives birth to her child, "It's a *good tired*."

The Apostle Paul must have felt like this, when he said, "My time has almost run out. Very soon now I will be on my way to heaven.

I have fought long and hard for my Lord, and through it all I have kept true to Him. And now the time has come for me to stop fighting and rest" (II TIMOTHY 4:66, 7 LIVING LETTERS).

That, is a *good tired*!

"It Isn't God's Book. It's Mine"

We were trying to impress upon our small son that the Bible is God's Book. He was leaving for Vacation Bible School one morning, proudly carrying his Bible. "This isn't God's Book," he announced. "It's mine." Saying the Bible is our book, possessively, is not an insult to God, rather, it is a compliment.

My father was dying. His wonderful mind was disturbed because of a deadly form of cancer affecting the marrow of his bones. In his depressed and emaciated condition, my father could still claim, "It's mine." Through his last conscious moments, he was comforted by the Twenty-Third Psalm: "The Lord is my shepherd; I shall not want. . . . Yea, though I walk through the valley of the shadow of death, I will fear no evil: for thou art with me . . ." (v. 1, 4 KJV).

This grand finale was not what we would have chosen for my father. We thought a life that was lived so unselfishly, so fully, should not end in this uncomfortable manner.

As I watched helplessly, I too claimed, "It's mine." I used these promises from Psalms, 103: "Like as a father pitieth his children, so the Lord pitieth them that fear him. For he knoweth our frame; he remembereth that we are dust. As for man, his days are as grass: as a flower of the field, so he flourisheth. For the wind passeth over it, and it is gone; and the place thereof shall know it no more. But the mercy of the Lord is from everlasting to everlasting upon them that fear him, and his righteousness unto children's children" (v. 13-17 KJV).

I saw my father draw his last gasping breath. All I could think was, "What a death!" Almost immediately, I had to add, "What a life!"

He had not reached three score and ten. I was consoled that life is not made up of just quantity, but also of quality. My father showed me that the Bible was "His Book."

"... You Die Too Soon"

I don't remember the setting, but one day Joe said, "I'm glad I wasn't made like Adam and Eve, when they were big. Then you die too soon." To most of us, death is always too soon.

Death made itself known to me when my mother died at twenty-four years of age. I was two years old and not able to comprehend the full blow, I'm sure. However, I believe this experience had something to do with my fear of death.

Heaven, too, was made real, but confusing. I knew my mother lay underneath that small brown stone which said *MOTHER*. I was told that my mother went to heaven.

How I argued mentally with my Sunday-school teacher a few years later! She said that when someone died he went up to heaven. To myself, I was insisting, "If my mother went down, that is where heaven must be!" Sitting on that little chair in Sunday school, I was having grown-up problems. Now, as a grown-up, I still have problems about some of these things.

There must be a happy medium between the love of living and the submission to dying. The desire for life is God given. Many of us struggled for our first breaths.

To be ready for dying is most important. If you are not, then truly, "... you die too soon."

SUNDRIES

We don't break our bread; we crack it.

". . . So Many Relief Pitchers"

Having four girls and one boy in our family is not exactly what is called balance. The one who takes the brunt of this deal is Joe.

I know there isn't one of his sisters (Rosie, Becky, Jenny, or Libby) he wouldn't fight for or pray for, but with three of them older than he, life sometimes becomes frustrating. He is advised on what he should say and informed on what he should not say. He is tipped off on when to make an appearance, and it is indicated when he should leave. I must add, in all fairness to his sisters, that many times he deserves it, because of his endless teasing.

I don't know which sisters were bossing him, when he said tauntingly, "Mother, I think it must do you a world of good not to be mother all the time. You have so many relief pitchers."

Of course, we are always in for trouble when we start telling others what to do, or what not to do. Unauthorized relief pitching is usually not appreciated. It is our responsibility to be our brother's keeper. However, what we consider to be our duty is many times out of bounds. To be our brother's conscience, his judge, or his shepherd, places us in positions that cannot be filled by relief pitchers.

My Grandmother

In a nostalgic mood, Libby was thinking about our old house, and came up with this solution: "We could cut this house in half and put it over there, and take half of our old house and put it over here."

The past and the present were not meant to be combined. We can only remember the past as it was, and enjoy the present as it is. I would love to introduce my children to my grandmother, and I would be happy if she could see my children, especially Rosie, who is her namesake. But her life will never have a repeat performance.

When she was fourteen years old, her mother died, leaving her with a mother's responsibility of raising two sisters and one brother younger than herself.

Later, in her own home, Grammy took in a sister, whose husband had left her before her baby was born. For twenty years or more, this was their home. A niece also made her home with my grandparents, because of her mother's death. There was her cousin, Harry, who came back from home-steading in Kansas to live with his Cousin Rose, too.

During the flu epidemic of World War I, her daughter died, leaving a one-and-one-half-year-old toddler and a six-day-old baby. Again, my grandmother filled a mother role. I, too, was a recipient of this unselfish love. My mother died when I was two, and she took care of me for two years, until my father remarried.

My uncle told me that there were times when she roomed and boarded three or four hired men. He also recalls the wages for one day (7 A.M. to 6 P.M.) at my grandfather's stone quarry were seventy-five cents, plus the noon meal, which meant twenty to thirty people had to be fed at noon.

In between all these activities, she reared six children of her own. My father was the second youngest. For forty-one years of her married life, she could not eat alone with her husband and children. Their table was always shared with others.

What do we remember most about my grandmother? Three cousins told me that calmness was her outstanding characteristic. My cousin Sam recalls how, on a rainy day, a croquet mallet slipped from his hands and crashed through the living room window. Because of her gentle reaction, he remembers her as a real understanding woman.

She spread herself over many lives and yet, somehow, none of us felt cheated. She was not too busy to pull down the kerosene light and read to the children, nor too tied up to bake little pies to thrill their hearts. Her Christ-like spirit flowed all around her.

Grandmother belonged in her setting. I would not want to change it. Her life from the past still speaks to us, and cannot help but influence the present and the future.

The Virus

If he had been in school today, Joe would have had an algebra test. But he has the virus, and is not without a few guilt pangs. He admitted to me this morning that yesterday in school he was just thinking that he hadn't missed any school this year. "I thought to myself," he said, "boy, that would be great, if I'd have off for my algebra test!"

Lying in his bed this morning, feverish and sick, he lamented, "I said I was sorry to God. I wonder if He did it to punish me?"

Our family had quite a bout with Asian flu, some years ago. My diary of the event went something like this: "Monday morning, 2 A.M. Rosie had fever of 102°."

One week later: "Monday, Joe had fever of 104°; Tuesday, I had fever of 102°; Thursday, Becky's temperature—104°; Saturday, Walter was warming up to 102°; Sunday, Joe started over again to which I raised the objection that no one had the right to be in bed twice until everyone had been there once."

We were headed into the third week of this monotonous routine. The checks we gave the doctor were numbered successively. Jenny was the most germ resistant of all. After the rest of us were feeling better, she too fell prey to this international bug.

We can learn through illness, and many times it is a blessing in disguise. However, not every virus we contract is sent as a punishment. Since our souls are wrapped up in human bodies, we all hurt and ache, chill and perspire. As mortals, we have not yet put on immortality.

"We Don't Break Our Bread ..."

Very often, I forget to take the bread from the freezer in time for it to thaw for dinner. This has become such a habit that Jenny remarked, "We don't break our bread; we crack it."

How did people exist before the days of frozen food? I could finish this chapter just naming the items we have in our freezer. Turkey, chicken, venison, beef, bread, nuts, buns, ice cream, pizza, vegetables—you name it; it's probably there.

We didn't do anything but buy most of this food. The vegetables were shelled, boxed, and frozen; the pizza was all made and packaged. With all this convenience, we lose a lot of fun and pleasure.

Our children have fond memories of going to a farm once a year to cut up beef. My husband was a butcher before he sold books, and I worked in a butcher shop for three years before we married. Between the two of us, we made a pretty good team. He boned the roasts and I rolled and tied them.

The winter night we went butchering, the whole family went along, and the farmer's whole family was there, too. We didn't know then that it was called togetherness. In the butchering kitchen, the wood fire was burning in the farmer's boiler. The room temperature was on the cold side, unless one was near the stove. With sweaters and galoshes, we were quite comfortable.

When we reached the rump and sirloin sections of the beef, Walter would pull out the tenderloin, slice it, and throw it into a hot pan. Did you ever eat filet mignon with your fingers? *Just* filet mignon? This was the highlight of the evening, and still gives us pleasure when we think of it.

We can't go back to the good old days. However, what we do today must replace that enjoyment. I'm not sure that cracking bread, instead of breaking it, will be remembered with warmth.

Nervous First Graders

"It seems I do my papers good at home, but not good in school," Libby commented. "Maybe I'm nervous," she diagnosed.

"Already?" I ask myself, "a child in first grade feeling nervous?"

Children are being pressured in school and in our homes. We parents think Johnny must be in the Little League, take trumpet lessons, study voice, practice wrestling, and do mountains of homework. This is not a life for children!

If we put children through adult routines, we reap disturbed children. We push them into walking and talking, and can't wait to send them to nursery school. Parents put their little people into grown-up clothes and expect them to act accordingly.

When I watch children walk home from school, I often marvel at the wonderful years of childhood. They have a franchise on these years and we are trying to spoil it.

I, as a mother, have been guilty of this. Many times I wanted my children to shine so I could add spark to my own pride, even at the expense of upsetting them. Pediatricians should not have to prescribe nerve pills, tranquilizers, and sleeping pills for physically healthy children, but they do.

It might be revealing to see a week of a child's life on a movie screen. I'm sure it would clear up some of our questions about nervous first graders.

A Study of Umbrellas

I was waiting in the car for our daughter, Becky, at the hospital where she works. It was a rainy day and umbrellas were all over the place. I began a study of how the people were using their umbrellas.

There was an intelligent looking couple, who were both carrying umbrellas, and a most unusual couple, who were evenly divided underneath the shelter of one umbrella. Young sweethearts, with arms around each other, had lots of room and some to spare.

One man really attracted my attention when, like a true gentleman, he reached for his companion's umbrella to carry it for her. "How nice," I thought.

This observation had scarcely registered in my mind, when I exclaimed, "Oh no!" The man was walking down the street well protected by the umbrella, and the lady was walking on the outside getting wet from the rain.

My exhaustive research ended abruptly when I saw two children with umbrellas walking home from school. They were carrying their umbrellas upside down in the rain, and using them to dip water out of the puddles.

No moral—just interesting!

"Last Minute, Smiley Customers"

"Here comes one of those last minute, smiley customers," Rosie groaned. It was a typical reaction from a clerk at closing time.

Rosie was raised in the store. She soon learned the gripes and the joys of the business. It's not just the last minute, smiley customers, but also the ones who call after hours or early in the morning.

Sunday business we discourage, but once in awhile we have the real "ox in the well" type of thing.

Early one Sunday morning, during a flu epidemic, the phone rang. "Hello?" A disturbed voice on the other end said, "This is John Doe from Saint Mark's Church. Say, we are in a fix . . . !" I cut in and objected, "I'm sorry, but Mr. Hackman is sick with the flu."

The caller persisted: "Well, we had our bulletins all printed and then one of our families had a baby, so we printed the congratulations on the back. But now, this morning, the minister was called to baptize the baby because they think he is dying. We don't want to hand out these bulletins; it might make the family feel bad. Would it be possible to pick up some more bulletins?" Sensing his urgency I said, "Hold on." I paraded back to my husband in my nightgown and told him the situation. "Well, you'll just have to go," he stated. "Hello, Mr. Doe," I said. "I'll go to the store and open it. Be there at 8:15."

Even though Rosie gripes and complains about the "last minute, smiley customers," my husband still contends: "Service is the rent that we pay for our stay here on earth."

Leaving the Nest

It was a small-family weekend at our home. Rosie was at college. Becky and Jenny were attending a youth retreat. "I don't like it at home without the girls," Libby pined. Even after Becky and Jenny came home, Libby still contended, "I'm still not happy. I want Rosie home." There is a feeling of completeness in seeing all seven chairs occupied. Then I can relax from the worry of wondering where each one is. However, Libby and I will both need to accept the fact that from here on, there will be many weekends, weeks, months, and semesters when we can take the big board out of the table.

How can I brace myself for the jolt? The lifeless telephones, mute door bells, empty chairs, and extra beds? I am struggling with knots in my apron strings, knots that I have tied myself. Instead of making a simple knot that would pull open nicely and easily, we sometimes make it too secure. In God's plan for families, there is a time for children to leave the nest, and there can be happiness in allowing this plan to be realized.

A friend of mine tells the following story: "When I was a child, my mother said, 'This is the best time of your life!' Again when I was a teen-ager in school, a young married woman, feeling the responsibility of marriage, told me, 'This is the best time of your life!' After I married, a young mother declared, 'You and your husband are free to go wherever you want to. This is the best time of your life!' One evening after I had tucked the children in bed, an elderly lady, who was then a grandmother, said to me, 'This is the best time of your life!' I am a grandmother now, and I think now is the best time of my life. I thank God every night that my grandchildren are in happy homes. They are wanted, and are being raised in the fear of the Lord. We've been blessed!"

What more could any mother ask?

"... No New Thing Under the Sun"

Libby is learning new math. So is her mother learning new math.

Her teacher told me that it is taught in cycles. What you don't catch on the first round, you might latch on to in the next. Instead of just learning the answer to three plus two, you are given the answer and you figure out the question. When you can figure out the answers and the questions, you have it.

Libby was trying some of her knowledge on her older sister, Jenny, when she asked, "How much is two plus two?" Slyly, Libby looked at her fingers and explained, "I'm not counting my fingers, I just want to make sure." We did the very same thing, when we studied old math. The Bible says: "... there is no new thing under the sun" (ECCLESIASTES 1:9, KJV).

I remember when the hemlines dropped about twenty years ago; it was called the new look—not really new, because our grandmothers wore dresses that skimmed their ankles. It was actually a return to the old.

The new morality that this generation is bragging about, Paul describes vividly in the first chapter of Romans: "Claiming themselves to be wise without God, they became utter fools instead" (ROMANS 1:22, LIVING LETTERS). "... always thinking of new ways of sinning and continually disobedient to their parents" (v. 30). "So it was that when they gave God up and would not even acknowledge Him, God gave them up to doing everything their evil minds could think of" (v. 28).

What I have tried to say in this book is not new either. It just has a more recent copyright.